Stephen Law was a postman before taking a degree in philosophy and holding a Junior Research Fellowship at the Queen's College, Oxford. He now teaches philosophy at Heythrop College, University of London. He has published a number of books including *The Philosophy Files*, *The Outer Limits* and *The Philosophy Gym*.

# THE
# XMAS FILES

*The Philosophy
of Christmas*

Stephen Law

PHOENIX

A PHOENIX PAPERBACK

First published in Great Britain in 2003
by Weidenfeld & Nicolson
This paperback edition published in 2004
by Phoenix,
an imprint of Orion Books Ltd,
Orion House, 5 Upper St Martin's Lane,
London WC2H 9EA

A CIP catalogue record for this book
is available from the British Library.

ISBN 0 75381 795 0

Printed and bound in Great Britain by
Clays Ltd, St Ives plc

*For Bill and Maureen*

# Acknowledgements

I am very grateful for comments from Rodas Irving, Mick O'Neill, Taryn Storey, Nigel Warburton and especially Richard Price.

# Contents

# Introduction

Christmas is one of the last great traditions that is shared by believers and non-believers alike in the West. At a time when tradition, particularly religious tradition, is on the wane, Christmas stands out as a great exception.

Christmas is also a particularly thought-provoking time of the year. In fact it raises a whole host of puzzles and dilemmas, from the trivial to the profound. Should you lie to Aunt Gertrude about that horrendous tie she bought you? Just how much should we be giving to the poor and needy at Christmas time? Is it morally acceptable to serve turkey on Christmas day?

The religious side of Christmas also raises some very deep questions. How is the Christmas message of peace to be understood? Is Christmas a festival that atheists can, in good conscience, celebrate? And is it really reasonable to suppose that Christ was both divinely conceived and born of a virgin?

Within these pages you will find me struggling with these and many other philosophical questions raised by the Christmas season. The book is made up of fourteen essays, each tackling a different topic. Some are fairly light-hearted; others are more serious. No background knowledge of philosophy is required at all. And the essays may be read in any order, so feel free to dip in and out as you choose.

# 1

## Wrapping the Presents

*Christmas is supposed to be a time for giving to others, including those less fortunate than us. But just how altruistic ought we to be? Indeed, do we ever really act selflessly? Aren't the acts of kindness so piously performed at Christmas really performed out of an ulterior motive? Deep down, are we all Scrooge?*

As the Christmas season approaches, we are reminded to think of others, and to put their interests before our own, at least momentarily. We are encouraged to dig a little deeper into our pockets, perhaps by dropping some money into a collection jar or setting up a direct debit to a charity. These actions are to be applauded.

Or are they? I am going to look at two interesting philosophical lines of argument, both of which finally conclude that our Christmas-inspired good deeds are often far from worthy. The first concludes that no one *ever* does anything other than out of self-interest, not even giving to the poor. The second suggests that while we may indeed give selflessly, what we give is, frankly, not enough.

## *Do we always act in our own interest?*

In the past, many philosophers, psychologists and econo-
mists have been drawn to psychological egoism, including,
perhaps most notably, the seventeenth-century philosopher Thomas Hobbes.[1] According to psychological egoism, every act we perform is done out of self-interest. We
always do whatever we perceive to be good for ourselves.
While its popularity may now have waned among
academics, the theory of psychological egoism still remains
popular among the general public.

It is, of course, rather a depressing theory. Most of us
would prefer to think of ourselves as, if not out-and-out
martyrs, then at least the type of person who occasionally
helps others at our own expense. Psychological egoism
denies this. Scratch the surface and we all turn out to be
repugnant and self-serving. We might pretend to act
selflessly, of course. We might even manage to convince
ourselves that we are putting the interests of others first. If
so, we are deluded. For the truth is that, deep down, we're
all as Scrooge-like as it is possible to be.

So why are people drawn to psychological egoism? At
first blush, it does have at least one very attractive feature:
simplicity. Psychological egoism provides a single, unify-
ing explanation for all human behaviour: self-interest.
Now, obviously, we do very regularly act in our own self-
interest. The psychological egoist notes this, and merely
extends the same kind of explanation to cover all our
deliberate actions.

## *Apparent counter-examples to psychological egoism*

Is psychological egoism true? On the face of it, no. I'm sure you can think of endless examples of seemingly selfless behaviour. Didn't Oskar Schindler save many Jewish lives at great risk to his own? Didn't Mother Teresa devote her life to helping relieve the suffering of others? Don't we see little acts of selflessness every day, when our car breaks down and we need a push, when a complete stranger stops what they are doing to help us pick up our shopping? Don't people place their hard-earned cash into the Christmas charity box? Isn't it just obvious that psychological egoism is false? We may not all be selflessly devoted to others, but don't we, on occasion, put their interests before our own?

Psychological egoists are, of course, well aware of such apparent counter-examples to their view. They insist that the altruistic explanation of these acts is too superficial. The real explanation lies elsewhere.

Take, for example, acts of charity. Hobbes seems to suggest that while charitable acts might look altruistic, the correct explanation for why people behave charitably is that they wish to demonstrate, either to others or themselves, their own power. 'Look!' they are saying. 'Not only can I afford to provide for myself – I'm even able to provide for others as well!'

According to the psychological egoist, then, we can be confident that the correct explanation for our behaviour is always egoistical, even if we cannot be entirely sure of precisely what that explanation might be.

## Is psychological egoism true?

So should we accept the claims of psychological egoism? No. In fact, psychological egoism is now largely discredited. One problem it faces is that the main justification for embracing it appears unacceptably circular. It's suggested that we should embrace psychological egoism because it always provides the best explanation of our behaviour. Certainly, it is always possible, with a little ingenuity, to come up with an egoistic explanation for almost anything we do. But just because such an explanation can be constructed doesn't guarantee that it is the correct, or even the most plausible, one. True, there are occasions where independent evidence shows that what seems to be done altruistically is done purely from selfish motives. If little Timmy puts money in the charity box, but then brags about it endlessly afterwards, and it's then found that his contribution was a worthless foreign coin, then we have good reason to prefer the egoistical explanation to the altruistic. But often there is no such evidence. In fact, often the evidence strongly supports the altruistic explanation. The claim that the egoistic explanation must still be the correct explanation even in these cases is, as it stands, quite unfounded.

There are other arguments for psychological egoism, however. Some, for example, point out that whenever we act altruistically, we still derive a sense of satisfaction from what we do. So, the argument goes, the reason that the action was performed was to produce that desired feeling.

This argument was demolished by the theologian and philosopher Bishop Butler.[2] Yes we get satisfaction from helping others, but it does not follow that this feeling is the primary motive: it may merely be a happy by-product. After all, if we only wanted to achieve the feeling of satisfaction, then what if that same feeling could be achieved simply by taking a pill? If what we really wanted was the feeling, then we could simply choose to take the pill and not trouble ourselves with the bothersome altruism. But of course we wouldn't take the pill. We really do want to help others.

But still, the egoists might say, when we help others at our own expense, we are nevertheless doing what we most *want* to do. You put that money in the Christmas charity box because you wanted to, didn't you? Schindler helped Jews escape the Nazis because he wanted to. But then he was acting out of self-interest. He was putting his own desires before those of anyone else.

This argument is also faulty. Yes, we help others because we want to. It does not follow that what we want to do is always in our own interest. Indeed, we may recognise that what we want to do is not in our own interest at all. Pointing out that Schindler helped others at his own expense because he wanted to does absolutely nothing to diminish the extraordinary selflessness of his actions. We can all agree that he did it because he wanted to without committing ourselves to the view that he acted selfishly.

Despite its deeply implausible character, psychological egoism still appeals to a certain sort of dinner-party conversationalist: the kind that likes to be provocative and to deflate people's opinions of themselves and others. They recognise in psychological egoism a position that cannot be refuted simply by wheeling out a few counter-examples in the form of Schindler and Mother Teresa. That leads them to think the position must be irrefutable, which it isn't.

## *How generous should we be?*

Assuming that we *are* able to act selflessly, how selfless should we be? Just how much cash should we give away? Are those few notes enough?

The commonsense view is that while it may be noble to give to those less fortunate, we are not duty-bound to give away large chunks of what we own. We think that someone who has worked hard throughout their life is, morally speaking, perfectly entitled to keep at least most of what they have, and to pass it on to their relatives. The rich may choose to give some of their wealth away, but they are not obliged to do so.

As we are focusing on Christmas, what would Jesus have to say about our festive generosity? When a rich man asked what he should do to inherit eternal life, Jesus told him to obey the commandments. When the man replied that he had observed them since his youth, Jesus said: 'One thing thou lackest: go thy way, sell whatsoever thou hast, and give to the poor, and thou shalt have treasure in heaven' (Mark 10: 21). The disciples were astonished at Jesus's words, and so he explained: 'Children, how hard it is for them that trust in riches to enter into the kingdom of God! It is easier for a camel to go through the eye of a needle, than for a rich man to enter into the kingdom of God' (Mark 10: 24–5).

These passages appear to be clear and unequivocal, and

more or less identical comments are also reported in Matthew and Luke. It does seem to be Jesus's view that the rich are very, very unlikely indeed to find themselves a place in the kingdom of Heaven. They should sell all they possess and give it to the poor.

If that is what Jesus thinks, then of course his view runs entirely counter to what the majority of us believe. His teaching is radical and revisionary – rather too radical and revisionary for most tastes.

Some religious commentators have suggested that we need to reinterpret Jesus. Perhaps it's not that difficult for a rich man to enter the kingdom of Heaven. For example, one or two commentators have raised the possibility that Jesus's 'eye of the needle' might have been a narrow gateway in the walls of Jerusalem through which a camel could pass, but with difficulty. There is, however, no evidence at all that such an 'eye of the needle' gate ever existed and this 'interpretation' looks suspiciously like a rather desperate attempt to find a loophole for the rich.

If we assume that Jesus really did want the rich to give their wealth to the poor, is his injunction unreasonable? The philosopher Peter Unger has developed a rather nice thought-experiment that seems, on the face of it, to support the view that Jesus's command is actually very reasonable indeed.

## Bob's Bugatti

Suppose Bob, a seventy-year-old engineer, has worked hard all his life and managed to amass $3 million. He keeps $3,000 in an account for emergencies and puts the rest into his retirement fund: an uninsurable vintage, mint-condition Bugatti automobile, which can be expected to appreciate in value at 20 per cent a year. There is a risk attached to placing all his savings in the car: what if some terrible accident should befall it? But still, Bob is prepared to take the risk. After all, if the car is written off, Bob will be able to get by, just.

Bob is now confronted with a terrible dilemma.

On a rural road near the garage where it's securely kept, Bob's gone for a careful drive in his Bugatti. At a certain point, he spies a shiny object. To inspect it, Bob parks his car in the only place convenient from where, directly, he can proceed on foot for a close encounter, a parking place that's just ten yards beyond the end of a certain trolley track. As it develops, when Bob walks over to the shiny object, he finds it's a switch that can be set two ways. And, as Bob observes, there's a trolley up the line that's barreling towards the switch's fork. As the switch is set, the trolley will go down the fork's opposite side, not the branch line leading to a spot near Bob's Bugatti. But, as Bob sees, on that side there's a young child trapped on the track. As he knows, Bob has two options: if he does nothing about the situation, the child will be killed, but he'll enjoy a comfortable retirement. If he changes the switch's setting, his second option, then while nobody's killed, after rolling down the vacant branch and beyond the track's end, the trolley will totally destroy Bob's uninsurable Bugatti, wiping out his entire retirement fund. Bob chooses the first option and, while the child is killed, he has a comfortable retirement.[3]

★

As Unger points out, when confronted with this case, we all think that Bob's behaviour is monstrous.

But now consider another case. Ray's situation is much like Bob's, except that Ray has been asked to contribute 99 per cent of all his assets to UNICEF's efficient, life-saving programme. Ray understands that, if he does so, thousands of children's lives will be saved. Ray would be left with $30,000 to his name (ten times more than Bob would have had). But Ray decides not to meet the request, and so thousands of children needlessly die.

In this case, most of us think Ray's position entirely reasonable. Ray would be left with ten times as much money as Bob would have had, and if he had acted, thousands of lives would have been saved, not just one. Yet most of us would consider Ray's behaviour far less reprehensible than Bob's.

But why? The answer, Unger suggests, is largely psychological. Bob is presented with the consequences of his failure to act in a very direct and dramatic fashion: a child will be crushed to death right before his eyes. For Ray, on the other hand, the children he could save are thousands of miles away and unknown to him. Ray may, perhaps, have seen some of the children on TV, but he is, to a much larger extent than Bob, psychologically insulated from the consequences of his inaction. That makes it much easier for him to do nothing. And, of course, Ray can also try to convince himself of the futility of giving away most of his wealth. After all, his contribution would be but a drop in the ocean compared to the amount needed to save *every* child's life.

But do these differences between the two cases really justify Ray's behaviour? Not according to Unger, who believes we have just as much moral obligation to save the distant, unseen child as we have to save the one right before us.

I am inclined to think Unger is correct about this. Suppose the cable connecting Bob's switch to the catastrophe is many thousands of miles long, rather than just a few yards. Also suppose that the trolley scene is conveyed to Bob on TV rather than being played out in front of him. Would Bob be under any less obligation to flip the switch and save the child? Would the distance and the circuitousness of the link between him and impending disaster let Bob off the hook?

Intuitively not. But then how can it make any difference whether the starving children that Ray's money can save are right there before his eyes or merely seen on a TV news report? How is that morally relevant to whether or not he should act?

Unger also rejects the futility excuse, and rightly so I think. If the futility excuse were good, then it would also excuse Bob's behaviour, for Bob could say, 'There are so many children dying needlessly every day: what real difference does it make whether or not I act to save this particular child's life?'

It is, in short, extremely difficult to justify discriminating between Bob's and Ray's cases in the way we do. In fact, Unger argues, it is just as bad, if not worse, for Ray to allow thousands of children to die as it is for Bob to let just one die.

## *Should I sell my house and give the proceeds to the poor?*

There is a more general moral we might draw. Most of us are not as well off as Bob and Ray, but still, most of us could easily afford to give away a substantial chunk of our assets and still get by. We are, relatively speaking, incredibly rich compared to those whose lives might be saved with our money. Yet, like Ray, we do nothing. In fact, most of us think we are entirely within our rights to do so. We're not doing anything wrong or bad.

But is that true? Aren't we, in fact, just as bad as Bob?

Personally, I haven't previously felt under any moral obligation to sell off my home and car and give the proceeds to UNICEF. But perhaps I am. Certainly, I'm having some trouble explaining why, by refusing to do so, I'm not just as bad as Bob. Rather than dropping a few coins in the charity box at Christmas, we should, perhaps, be asking ourselves whether we don't have a moral duty to do much, much more.

---

1 See Thomas Hobbes, *Leviathan* (London: Penguin, 1981).
2 'Fifteen Sermons Preached at the Rolls Chapel' in *The Works of Bishop Butler*, ed. J.H. Bernard (London: Macmillan, 1900), Sermons I and XI.
3 Peter Unger, *Living High and Letting Die* (Oxford: OUP, 1996), p. 136.

# 2

## Aunt Gertrude's Hideous Tie

*It's Christmas Day and Aunt Gertrude has just handed you an attractively wrapped oblong box. Ripping off the paper, you discover that, for the tenth year running, she has given you a hideous tie. You wouldn't be seen dead in it. Yet Aunt Gertrude looks expectantly into your eyes, waiting for some sign of approval. What do you do? Do you hide your disappointment and lie, saying how lovely the tie is, and how it will go perfectly with that new shirt you've just bought? Or do you tell the truth?*

*Philosophical opinion is divided.*

### Kant's advice

The eighteenth-century philosopher Immanuel Kant would say: tell the truth. According to Kant, morality takes the form of certain strict and absolute imperatives: do not kill; do not steal, and so on. They are principles that reason demands we obey, and they admit no exceptions whatsoever. Do not lie is, according to Kant, one of these absolute principles. It is your moral duty not to lie. Ever. So you must tell Aunt Gertrude the truth – or at least, you must not lie: perhaps you might try distracting her attention with an offer of a cup of tea, but if that doesn't work you have no option but to tell the truth or remain silent, which will lead her to guess the truth.

But, of course, the result of not lying in this case is likely to be a very upset aunt. She is highly strung and you know she will take the truth badly. In all probability she will leave your home in tears. Shouldn't you take these consequences into account?

Not according to Kant, who insists that the results of an action have absolutely nothing to do with its moral probity. Of course, the consequences of not lying could, in some circumstances, be very serious indeed. Upsetting Aunt Gertrude is bad enough. But what about the mad axeman who breaks into your house and demands to know where your children are hiding? It seems the only way to save them is to put him off the scent by lying. What should you do?

Tell the truth! says Kant. The consequences are, morally speaking, completely irrelevant!

## *The consequentialist's advice*

Most of us, of course, are aghast at the suggestion that we should tell the truth in such circumstances. In the case of the mad axeman, at least, a consequentialist approach seems much more appropriate. Consequentialists insist that, if you want to know what you ought to do when confronted with a moral dilemma, then figure out what the likely outcome will be. But then, how should we assess the value of one outcome over another?

One of the simplest versions of consequentialism says that you should calculate which course of action is likely to produce the most happiness. This is the position of John Stuart Mill and is called utilitarianism.

So what would Mill have to say about Aunt Gertrude's tie? It depends. According to a simple utilitarian view, you should do whatever will produce the happiest outcome. On the face of it, the right course of action would appear to be to lie. For then Aunt Gertrude will leave your home feeling happy, rather than upset. The world will be a happier place than it would otherwise have been.

But, of course, calculating which course of action is likely to result in the most happiness is not as straightforward as it might appear. Whilst telling Aunt Gertrude the truth might make her less happy in the short term, in the long run she may be happier (perhaps she suspects you don't like her presents, which is causing her considerable anguish, and perhaps, by telling her the truth, that anguish could be removed). And you may be happier too: you won't have to keep up this charade year after year and you may receive gifts that you genuinely like rather than ones that embarrass you.

## *Happiness and deceit*

There is another worry you might have about the utilitarian approach. In the film *The Truman Show*, the central character lives out his life, from birth, within an idyllic world built entirely for him. Everyone he has ever spoken to, including the people he believes are his parents, is an actor. Every aspect of his day-to-day life is stage-managed and relayed to the millions who watch *The Truman Show* on TV. Truman doesn't realise that his life is a soap opera; he thinks his world is genuine. Truman's perfect, all-American, apple-pie life does make him happy – at least until he begins to suspect the truth. But his happiness is created by a huge lie and his world is nothing but a charade. We recognise that, while Truman might feel quite content within his idyllic bubble, contrived happiness is not enough. It is wrong to treat Truman in that way. It seems that there are, morally speaking, more important things than happiness. If feeling happy is all that ultimately matters, then why not spend our lives in a state of permanent, drug-induced euphoria?

Aunt Gertrude might, indeed, feel happier if you lie to her. But in lying to her, aren't you treating her the same way that the producers of *The Truman Show* treated Truman (if on a smaller scale, of course)? Is happiness born of deceit a happiness worth having?

You might also consider how you would want to be treated if you were in Gertrude's position. Would you want to be lied to? I would guess not. Certainly, I would much prefer to know the truth: I would want to know that you hated my gifts, so that I could do something about it. If that is how you would wish to be treated, shouldn't you treat Gertrude the same way? Shouldn't you tell her the truth?

It's a tough call.

# 3

## Christmas and God

*If Christmas is what it claims to be — the day on which the son of God was born — then that raises, of course, the biggest question of all: does God exist? For many, belief in God is a matter of faith, not reason. They insist that we should just believe, whatever the arguments and the evidence might suggest (indeed, perhaps despite what the evidence and arguments might suggest). But are there good grounds for supposing that God exists?*

What sort of being is God? What is he like? Whilst God is deeply mysterious, he is not so very mysterious that we cannot be fairly confident of some of his properties. In fact, at least as he is traditionally conceived, the God of the Jews, Christians and Muslims must have, at the very least, each of the following three attributes.

First, God, if he exists, is supremely benevolent. He is, in other words, wholly good. Christians, in particular, believe that God loves and cares for us as if we were his children and that he gave us his son to redeem us.

Second, God is omnipotent or all-powerful; there are no limitations to what God can do. He can part seas, bring the dead back to life and create an entire universe.

Third, God is omniscient. He knows everything, including our innermost thoughts and feelings. God sees all.

This is, of course, a very bare character sketch and no doubt God has many more properties than just the three rather abstract ones listed here. But we can be confident that God, as traditionally understood, is omnipotent, omniscient and supremely benevolent. God can no more avoid being omnipotent than a triangle can avoid being three-sided. A being that possessed only two of these properties – that was, for example, all-powerful and all-knowing but not all-good – might be *a* god. But, by definition, he would not be *the* God with a capital G.

Armed with this little character-sketch, let's now turn to the question of whether such a being actually exists.

One of the most popular of all the arguments for the existence of God is the cosmological argument. It is also one of the oldest arguments for God's existence: both Plato and Aristotle present a form of it. There are a number of different versions, but the following is fairly typical.

## *The cosmological argument*

Where did the universe come from? Why does it exist? Indeed, why is there anything at all? According to most scientists, the universe exists because of the Big Bang: the mind-wrenchingly cataclysmic explosion in which matter and energy, and indeed time and space, were created.

But to appeal to the concept of the Big Bang in order to explain why there is anything at all really only postpones the mystery. For of course, this scientific explanation of why the universe exists leads us inexorably on to the question: and why did the Big Bang occur?

After all, things don't just happen, do they? Suppose that there is a mystery explosion at a chemical factory. Investigators would be unlikely to conclude that this explosion just happened. They would suppose, and with good reason, that the explosion must have had some cause, whether or not they happen to know what the cause is. The same, many would argue, is true of the Big Bang. It's far more reasonable to suppose that it was the result of something than to believe it just happened for no reason at all.

It is at this point that God enters the picture. God, many would say, caused the Big Bang. He provides the best explanation we have for why the universe exists. That's why it is reasonable to believe in God.

Of course, a proponent of the cosmological argument can admit that, while this argument might give us good grounds for supposing that God exists, these grounds are not absolutely conclusive. 'I might be wrong,' they may say, 'but it is, on balance, more reasonable to believe in God than not to.'

As I say, the cosmological argument is highly popular, and has appealed to a number of important theist philosophers, including St Aquinas, Spinoza and Leibniz.

But is the argument cogent? Does it give us good, if not conclusive, grounds for supposing that God exists?

## *The regress problem*

Notoriously, the argument appears to prove rather more than most theists want. What motivates the introduction of God is the thought that everything requires a cause and explanation. That leads us to suppose that the universe requires a cause and explanation, which in turn leads us on to the thought that there must be a God. At this point, the theist wishes to stop, happy to arrive at their chosen destination. But, unfortunately, the principle with which we began – the principle that everything requires a cause and explanation – leads them inexorably on. For if everything requires an explanation, then of course, so does God. If we are justified in introducing something to explain the existence of the universe, then we are also justified in introducing something to explain the existence of God (a second God, perhaps?) And in fact we won't be able to stop there, either, for whatever explains the existence of God will in turn require something that explains its existence (a third God?), and so on ad infinitum. We have generated an infinite regress.

You could think of the principle that everything requires a cause and explanation as the logical 'train' that pulls the cosmological argument along. We step aboard the train, hoping that it will lead us to our selected destination: the existence of God. The problem is that while the train may lead us to our chosen station, it won't let us off. The doors remain firmly locked and we watch helpless as we are whizzed off to the next station. And then the next. And then the next. We have embarked on a journey without end.

The real problem with the cosmological argument – the reason why it generates an endless chain of causes and explanations – is that it takes for granted what it's supposed to explain. At each step, the mystery of why there is anything at all is not actually dealt with. By adding God on to the beginning of the universe we succeed only in postponing the question of why there is something rather than nothing.

But perhaps the cosmological argument can be salvaged. One popular move is to insist that the key principle on which the argument hinges – that everything has a cause and explanation – simply needs tweaking. In the revised version of the argument, everything has a cause and explanation except God. God is the one exception to the rule. As everything but God requires a cause and explanation, it is reasonable to suppose that God exists as the cause and explanation of the universe. But as God himself requires no cause and explanation, when we arrive at God, we reach the end of the line.

## Hume's elephant

This is an ingenious 'fix'. But this revised version of the cosmological argument runs into difficulties of its own. The following analogy may help to explain why.

The ancient Hindus were perplexed by the question of how everything is supported. After all, most solid objects will fall if they are not supported by something else. Release a pebble and it will tumble until it finally hits a support: the Earth. But that raises the question of what holds the Earth up. If everything requires a support, then the Earth too requires a support. So what supports it?

The Hindu answer was imaginative. They supposed that the Earth rides on the back of a great, cosmic turtle. Now this suggestion might, for a moment, seem to solve the puzzle. But only for a moment. For of course, the cosmic turtle merely postpones the mystery. For now we face the question: what holds the turtle up?

So the Hindus added a second creature – a great elephant – to hold up the first. The Earth sits on the back of a turtle, which is in turn perched on the back of an elephant. The Hindus simply stopped at the elephant. They didn't add a third animal to support it, and then a fourth and fifth and so on ad infinitum. They made the elephant the exception to the rule.

But of course, this just raises the question: why make the elephant the exception to the rule? Why not make the turtle the exception? In fact, why not make the Earth the exception and dispense with the animals altogether?

The revised version of the cosmological argument runs into similar problems. Once we start making exceptions to the rule that everything has a cause and explanation, what reason is there to make God the exception rather than the universe? As the eighteenth-century philosopher David Hume pointed out, we have been given no more reason to suppose that God exists than we have to suppose the great elephant exists.

'If we stop and go no farther, why go so far? Why not stop at the material world? How can we satisfy ourselves without going on ad infinitum? And after all, what satisfaction is there in that infinite progression? Let us remember the story of the Indian philosopher and his elephant. It was never more applicable than to the present subject.'[1]

Of course, this is not to say that it's curtains for the cosmological argument. It may be that the argument can, again, be bolstered. We might, for example, try to justify the claim that God is the only thing that can reasonably be considered an exception to the rule. But, as it stands, the cosmological argument fails. It gives us no reason at all to suppose that God exists.

## *The argument from design*

Just because one particular argument for the existence of God has been found to fail, that doesn't imply that belief in God is not reasonable. For there may be other, better arguments that can be mustered in support of that belief.

Like the cosmological argument, the argument from design also appears in a number of different versions. Here is the theologian William Paley's version.

Look at the eye. Look at the intricate way in which it is constructed to fulfil a particular function: that of allowing the creature attached to it to see. Surely the suggestion that blind natural forces all by themselves somehow managed to produce such an ingeniously constructed object is too much to swallow. Surely it is far more plausible to suppose that the eye is a product of some form of intelligence, but an intelligence that must far exceed our own. It seems plausible, then, to suppose that the eye's designer is God.

Since the development of Darwin's theory of natural selection, this particular version of the argument from design has become far less popular. For, of course, Darwin managed to explain exactly how an object such as an eye might evolve quite naturally, without any sort of supernatural help. As our knowledge of how the universe operates has expanded, the plausibility of the suggestion that only God can make something like a tree or an eye has diminished. Yes, there are gaps in our knowledge (in particular, we do not yet fully understand how DNA – required for Darwinian natural selection to occur – emerged in the first place). But these gaps are closing all the time, and it seems increasingly likely that an entirely satisfactory naturalistic explanation of the richness and complexity of life will finally emerge. It appears that, in terms of explaining how life on Earth emerged, appeals to supernatural beings like God will finally be rendered surplus to requirements.

However, there are other versions of the argument from design that, rather than being undermined by modern scientific discoveries, seem actually to be supported by them. Here, for example, is what I call the intelligent design argument.

## *The intelligent design argument*

Consider the laws of nature that govern how matter and energy behave within the universe. It seems that these laws might have been different. Take, for example, the forces of gravitational attraction. They might have been slightly stronger than they actually are or they could have been much weaker. In fact, we can think of the laws of nature as being set by a series of giant levers that can be placed in an infinite number of different positions. As I say, the gravity lever could have been set a little higher or much lower than it is. Yet the levers happen to be set in just *this* position.

Now we could, of course, insist that the levers of the universe were set at random, quite arbitrarily. But, some theists maintain, this is extraordinarily unlikely. For if the levers had been set even slightly differently, then a stable universe capable of sustaining and producing life and, indeed, conscious beings like ourselves, would not have emerged. For example, if the lever governing gravitational attraction had been set just a little bit higher, then the universe would have collapsed back on itself milliseconds after creation. The Big Bang would immediately have been followed by a Big Crunch, annihilating everything.

Now the fact that the levers should happen to be set just so, *purely by chance*, would appear to be a cosmic fluke of outrageous proportions. The reasonable thing to believe, then, according to the proponent of the intelligent design argument, is that the levers were not set at random, but were knowingly and deliberately positioned with great precision to produce a stable universe that would bring forth life. An intelligent being deliberately set up the universe in this way for us. That being is God.

This version of the design argument has become increasingly popular, and is supported by some very eminent theologians and philosophers of religion. In my view, it is the best argument for the existence of God there is.

But, even so, I think the argument, as it stands, is flawed. Here is one problem with it: at best, the argument makes rational only the belief that the universe possesses some sort of intelligent, mindful designer. It is one step further to the conclusion that this designer is God: a being that is omnipotent, omniscient and supremely benevolent. Why suppose the designer is God? In particular, why suppose that the universe's designer is good – that he is the loving and caring creator that we take him to be?

In fact, when we examine the universe more closely, we

appear to find compelling evidence that our creator, if he exists at all, is, at best, indifferent to our suffering and, at worst, downright sadistic.

## The problem of evil

The problem of evil is undoubtedly the best-known and probably the most powerful of all the arguments against the existence of God. It runs as follows.

We know that, whatever else may be true of God, according to the major world religions he is omnipotent, omniscient and supremely benevolent. But now take a look around the world: is it the kind of world such a being would create? There are wars and famines, earthquakes and floods, all of which cause humans immense suffering. And there are diseases too. Why would a God who supposedly loves and cares for us as if we were his children choose to inflict cancer, tooth decay, multiple sclerosis and the Black Death upon us in such an apparently indiscriminate manner?

Of course, it's not just humans that suffer. Animals were suffering for millions of years before humans even made an appearance on the face of the planet. Countless generations of creatures writhing in torment, dying the most excruciating deaths, and for what purpose? If God is all-powerful, then surely he could have created a world with at least much less suffering in it. And as God is also supremely benevolent, surely he would have created such a world, if he exists. Indeed, he would, presumably, have created a world much more like heaven is supposed to be.

The inescapable conclusion would appear to be that

God does not exist. There may be *a* god. But he isn't *the* God – that's to say, God as the Judaeo-Christian and Muslim traditions understand him.

This is an ancient puzzle for those who believe in God. Epicurus identified the problem even before the birth of Christ. He put it as follows: 'Is God willing to prevent evil, but not able? Then he is not omnipotent. Is he able, but not willing? Then he is malevolent. Is he both able and willing? Then whence the evil? Is he neither able nor willing? Then why call him God?'[2] A great many theologians have struggled with the problem that Epicurus raises. Some have managed to devise fairly ingenious solutions. But it's unclear whether any of these solutions really work.

## *The free-will defence*

One of the best-known attempts to solve the problem of evil is to suggest that what suffering there is in the world is actually our own fault, not God's. God gave us free will. We are not mere puppets dancing helplessly on God's strings but free agents capable of independent thought and action. Unfortunately, we sometimes choose to do the wrong thing, to start wars, for example. What evil there is in the world is the result of our free will.

Of course, God could have made us automata that always blindly do the right thing, but it is better that we have free will. Because God is good, he made us free, despite the fact that, by making us free, he gave us the power to create such suffering.

Does the free-will defence deal with the problem of

evil? It does, perhaps, succeed in explaining some of the suffering we see around us: the suffering that we cause. But one very obvious limitation of the free-will defence is that it is unable to explain a great deal of the other difficulties that we endure. It cannot explain the suffering caused by natural catastrophes such as earthquakes. Nor can it explain naturally occurring illnesses such as multiple sclerosis and cancer. And, of course, it fails to account for the many millions of years of suffering in the animal kingdom that occurred before our appearance on the earth. If there is a God, all this suffering is his responsibility, not ours.

## *Blame it on the devil*

Theists sometimes attempt to deal with the problem of evil by suggesting that what evil there is in the world is the work not of God, but the devil. The devil, a fallen angel, is a being of very considerable guile and power. Natural disasters and cancer are his handiwork, not God's.

The suggestion that natural evil can be blamed on the devil is flatly contradicted by one passage in the Bible: 'I form the light, and create darkness: I make peace, and create evil: I the Lord do all these things.' (Isa. 45: 7.) But still, perhaps not everything in the Bible is true. Perhaps natural disasters are the devil's work.

If evil is the work of the devil, does that mean God is blameless? Only if it is not within God's power to prevent the devil doing such despicable things. If God has to watch helplessly while the devil tortures us, then God certainly can't be held responsible for that torture. But, of course, we know that God is not helpless to prevent the devil's handiwork because, compared to the power of an omnipotent being, the devil's powers are, frankly, laughable. God versus the devil is really no contest at all; in fact it's infinitely less of a contest than Mike Tyson versus the man from the Mister Muscle advert. God could so very easily prevent all the suffering that the devil causes. So why doesn't he?

## 'No pain, no gain'

Of course, suffering can have a positive side. Sometimes, when someone has been through an awful ordeal – a serious illness, perhaps – they are strengthened and enriched by the experience. Suffering can be character building. It can be something we learn from.

So while God inflicts suffering on us, perhaps he does not do so pointlessly. Perhaps it is, in the end, for our own good. No pain, no gain.

Does this suggestion really deal with the problem of evil? I think not. To begin with, you might wonder why God didn't give us stronger, more fully developed characters to begin with. Why the needless agony? And even if suffering is the unavoidable price we must pay, it's difficult to understand why God dispenses suffering in the way he does. Why do mass-murdering dictators live out their lives in luxury? Why do kind and lovely people endure horrendous diseases? It is, to say the least, hard to comprehend how the seemingly random distribution of suffering in the world could really be all for the best.

On the other hand, perhaps the suffering wouldn't be good for us if it weren't seemingly random. If there appeared to be some purpose and order to it, would that maybe undermine its character-building effect?

This does seem to stretch belief, however. When we wish to build our children's characters, do we do so by randomly flogging some of them mercilessly for no reason at all while handing out presents to others irrespective of how despicably they might have behaved? Obviously not. Rather than building children's characters, this is rather more likely to break them. Rather than producing virtuous, well-adjusted individuals, we would probably end up with a bunch of psychopaths. Odd, then, that God should choose to inflict this rather unorthodox method of character building on us.

## 'God works in mysterious ways'

It can be tempting to appeal to God's mysteriousness in order to deal with the puzzle raised by suffering. God, we know, works 'in mysterious ways'. Given our limited intelligence, we can't be expected to make sense of everything he does, can we? Perhaps the suffering we endure is ultimately all for the best. It's just that, being mere humans, we can't see how.

At this point, the theist really is just admitting defeat. They are admitting that, despite the fact that the suffering doesn't seem to be consistent with the existence of God, nevertheless it might be. Well, yes, it might be. But that's not to deny that the evidence does, on the face of it, strongly support the view that there is no God.

After all, we can say the same about almost any belief, no matter how silly – 'But still, it *might* be true.' There *might* be fairies at the bottom of the garden. The moon *might* be made of concrete (perhaps there's been a huge conspiracy by NASA to cover up the truth). Indeed, the Belgians *might* turn out to be the secret rulers of the universe. That's not to deny that the available evidence very strongly suggests otherwise.

## *A non-good God?*

The problem of evil constitutes a powerful argument against the existence of God. The universe may have a creator. It may even show signs of intelligent design. The real difficulty facing believers is to explain how this designer could possibly be what they mean by 'God'.

Probably the easiest way for a theist to solve the problem of evil is simply to give up one of the attributes traditionally assigned to God. We could insist, for example, that while God is all-powerful and all-knowing, he is not all-good.

In fact, when we turn to the Old Testament, it does seem to bear this suggestion out. The God of the Old Testament appears to behave rather more like a mafia boss than our loving creator. He singles out one particular people as 'his', and controls them largely by fear. He demands sacrifices. He leads them in tribal wars and shows no mercy – demanding that even women and children should be put to the sword. He conducts bizarre loyalty tests (God instructed Abraham to sacrifice his only son), has temper tantrums and is vindictive, inflicting ridiculously cruel and over-the-top punishments that can extend even to a transgressor's distant family and beyond.

Does this sound like the behaviour of a supremely benevolent being? Not to me. We can solve the problem of evil at a stroke by simply admitting that God is not all-good.

## *The problem of good*

So is there an evil God, then? That suggestion runs into a problem analogous to the problem of evil: the problem of good. For there clearly is a great deal of good in the world, more good than an entirely evil God would allow. As those who believe in a good God run into the problem of evil, so those who believe in an evil God run into the problem of good.

Of course, just as theists try to show how what evil there might seem to be in the world is actually consistent with God's goodness, someone who believed in the existence of a supremely evil deity might try to defend their belief by insisting that what good there is in the world is actually entirely consistent with his depravity.

Why, for example, if God is cruel, does he allow some people to live out their entire lives in luxury, without a care in the world? Why doesn't he torture them instead? Because their comfort makes the rest of us feel *even more* miserable. *Hello!* magazine and *Lifestyles of the Rich and Famous* are all part of God's master plan to make the world a living hell.

But what about the good that people do? Their selfless behaviour? The love they feel towards each other? If God is entirely evil, why does he let us do these good things? The answer, perhaps, is that God gave us free will. By giving us a combination of free will and largely weak and selfish characters, God succeeded in making the world far more hellish than it would otherwise be. Through free will, God can make us agonise endlessly about what we should do. And he can be sure that, because we know we are able to do otherwise, we will feel truly awful when we do wrong. Of course, as a consequence of our having free will, we will occasionally do good. But the little bit of good that we do is more than offset by the misery free will brings.

Of course, this free-will defence of an evil God seems rather desperate and unconvincing. But then what of the same defence of a good God? You can see almost every move made by a theist in defence of their belief in a good God can be mirrored just as effectively by someone who believes in an evil God. The truth is, naturally, that all these defensive moves are rather feeble.

If the intelligent-design argument really does establish that we have an intelligent creator, perhaps the most sensible thing to believe is that he isn't all good, and that he isn't all evil. God is somewhere in between. He is, perhaps, simply indifferent to our suffering, like the child who plays at burning ants with a magnifying glass. His aim is not to make us suffer. It's just that he doesn't much care if we do.

## A mystery

Is it reasonable to believe in God? Are there good grounds for supposing that he exists? There may be. However, most of the more popular arguments turn out, at least in their simplest versions, to be pretty poor. And there is also an extremely powerful argument against the existence of

God (if only as he is traditionally conceived). Belief in God does not, prima facie, appear to be particularly reasonable.

Still, for those who believe that God exists – which would obviously include anyone who believes that at Christmas God became man – these arguments are ultimately irrelevant. Belief in God, they say, is a matter of faith, not reason.

Of course, we still haven't disposed of the question of why there is anything at all. When I go out for a walk at night and stare up at the stars in a quiet moment of contemplation, I am consistently struck by the question: 'Where did all this come from?' The question remains as profound and deeply puzzling as ever. Indeed, it would appear to be a question that it is in principle impossible to answer. For whatever we might point to in order to explain why there is something rather than nothing will of course just become another part of the total 'something' that needs to be explained.

But while we can acknowledge that there is a mystery about why there is anything at all, it is, at best, unclear how the existence of God provides any sort of solution. The appeal to God seems, not to solve the puzzle, but merely to sweep it under the carpet.

---

1 David Hume, *Dialogue Concerning Natural Religion*, Part IV, ed. Norman Kemp Smith (London: Penguin paperback edition, 1990) pp. 161–2.

2 Hume presents Epicurus's argument in his *Dialogue Concerning Natural Religion*, ibid.

# Christmas Card Kitsch

*Every year we send millions of cards to people whom we often scarcely know or even like, insisting that, nevertheless, we 'hope to see them soon'. Increasing numbers of these cards are accompanied by a 'round robin' – a cheery description of our family's past year. In these and innumerable other ways we enter into the 'Christmas spirit'. Here, Joseph and Mary thrash out some of the philosophical issues surrounding the annual swapping of cards.*

A domestic scene: Joe is sat on the sofa reading the paper while his wife, Mary, writes the Christmas cards. Their living room is festooned with paper chains, which Mary has hung that morning. Their fireplace sports all sorts of Christmas paraphernalia: cards, tinsel, stockings, baubles. Pride of place goes to an illuminated nativity scene. Joe looks up from his paper and examines the room. Then he looks at Mary, busy writing her cards.

JOE: Honestly, why do people waste their time sending these endless pieces of card through the post every year? After all, most of the people sending them aren't even Christians. You're not a Christian, are you?

MARY: You know I'm not.

JOE: So why are you sending Christmas cards?

MARY: We have this conversation every year.

JOE: But the question is still a good one, isn't it?

MARY: Look, if it wasn't for cards and Christmas many families would drift apart. The card I am writing at the moment is to your brother. Without my card, you wouldn't hear from each other at all most years. I think sending Christmas cards is a good thing, whether or not you're a Christian. It's all part of the Christmas spirit.

Joe gets up and walks over to the table where Mary is busy scribbling. He inspects some of her cards.

JOE: Hmm. But then why these silly, sentimental cards? Look at them! What have they got to do with the birth of Christ? Nothing. Kittens in bowler hats. Victorian scenes. Mountains. *Traction engines*, for goodness sake!

MARY: I think they look nice. You're just being stuffy.

C. S. Lewis would have agreed with Joseph. 'What in heaven's name is the idea of everyone sending everyone else pictures of stage-coaches, fairies, foxes, dogs, butter-flies, kittens, flowers, etc?' he wrote.[1] He has a point. If Christmas is a celebration of Christ's birth, then why all these ridiculously inappropriate images?

Still, as C. S. Lewis elsewhere admits, three things go by the name of Christmas: first, a religious festival; second, a holiday and occasion for merriment; and third, what Lewis calls the 'commercial racket'.[2] But then why shouldn't you send cards wishing others much merriment on their Christmas holiday? There is nothing at all hypocritical in that, surely? And if the senders aren't Christian, then why not send cards with kittens and traction engines on the front? Surely, for non-Christians who only want to wish others a happy holiday, cards with kittens and coaches are rather more appropriate than nativity scenes. And as Mary points out, Christmas cards perform a very useful social function by keeping family and friends in touch.

## *Kitsch and sentimentality*

Still, while kittens and stagecoaches might not be inappropriate, perhaps there's still something objectionable about a lot of the paraphernalia that surrounds Christmas, much of which is often highly kitsch and sentimental. As Mary continues to stuff envelopes, Joe picks up one of the gaudier cards. It depicts a bowler hat containing some snow-sprinkled kittens.

JOE: But the *sentimentality*! It's all so tacky!

MARY: What's wrong with being a little sentimental now and then?

JOE: Well, take these awful round robins you insist on slipping into the envelopes along with the cards. They're sentimental because they distort the truth.

MARY: They do?

JOE: They most certainly do. When you wrote your round robin, you carefully edited out the unpleasant stuff. You're presenting a glossy, touchy-feely version of our family's year.

MARY: But what about Granny's death? That's in there, isn't it? And that wasn't pleasant.

JOE: True. But you've airbrushed out the long periods of pain, her anguish, the guilt we felt about leaving her in that care home. Your version of what happened has been entirely sanitised.

MARY: You're just being your usual cold, cynical self. There's nothing wrong with focusing on the good, just for a change. So what if I'm being a little sentimental? I think people will be touched.

Like Joe, many people are deeply suspicious about Christmas kitsch and sentimentality. It tends to bring out a combination of sarcasm and snobbery. 'Look!' we say, pointing to the snow-flecked kittens in the bowler hat. 'How *awful*!' we snigger. 'How *tasteless*!'

But perhaps Mary is right. Perhaps Joe is guilty of being a cynical old snob. For what harm does a little kitsch and sentimentality really do?

Well, perhaps some harm. In *The Unbearable Lightness of Being*, Milan Kundera explains what kitsch originally meant:

> 'Kitsch' is a German word born in the middle of the sentimental nineteenth century, and from German it entered all Western languages. Repeated use, however, has obliterated its original metaphysical meaning: kitsch is the absolute denial of shit, in both the literal and the figurative senses of the word; kitsch excludes everything from its purview which is essentially unacceptable in human existence.[3]

When we enter a world of kitsch, we enter a world in which 'everyone acts as though [shit] did not exist'.[4] We communally erect a façade of faux-loveliness in front of real life, a façade designed to hide the truth. We collectively pretend. Kundera focuses on the use of kitsch within totalitarian communist regimes: the colourful May Day parades, the happy beaming faces, the children playing – imagery designed to obliterate any trace of unpleasant reality.

> Whenever a single political movement corners power, we find ourselves in the realm of *totalitarian kitsch*. When I say 'totalitarian', what I mean is that everything that infringes on kitsch must be banished for life: every display of individualism (because a deviation from the collective is a spit in the eye of the smiling brother-hood); every doubt (because anyone who starts doubting details will end by doubting life itself); all irony (because in the realm of kitsch everything must be taken seriously) . . . In this light, we can regard the gulag as a septic tank used by totalitarian kitsch to dispose of its refuse.[5]

Of course, I'm not suggesting that Christmas is comparable to the worst excesses of a totalitarian regime. But it seems to me that, particularly since Victorian times, the world of Christmas has become a world of kitsch. It's a sanitised place filled with children's laughter, glitter, tinsel and hearty good-humour. It's the world of the snow-flecked kittens and cosy Victorian fireside scenes; the world as it appears in films like Capra's *It's a Wonderful Life*. It's a vision of life that features in round robins. A place where everyone works desperately to sustain the illusion by pretending very hard that, as Kundera puts it, shit does not exist.

But then why shouldn't we pretend, at least for a week or so? Why not engage in a little escapist fantasy now and then? To repeat Mary's question: what real harm does it do?

## *The dangers of sentimentality*

Charles Dickens wrote about Christmas that it is 'a good time: a kind, forgiving, charitable, pleasant time: the only time I know of in the long calendar of the year, when men and women seem by one consent to open their shut-up hearts freely, and to think of other people below them as if they really were fellow-passengers to the grave, and not another race of creatures bound on other journeys'.[6] Few of us would wish to disagree with that, at least as a prescription of what Christmas should be like. But Dickens' own portrayals of Christmas and the Christmas spirit are often accused of being overly sentimental, and perhaps damagingly so.

For example, Dickensian sentimentality about the poor might cause us to have false beliefs about the reality of poverty, which could in turn lead to ineffective action in dealing with it. The philosopher Ira Newman outlines the charge as follows:

Dickens's novel *A Christmas Carol*, for instance, presents false views of the poor (their plight is entirely attributed to an immoral economic system, with surprisingly little responsibility given to their own character flaws); false views of moral improvement (Scrooge's miraculous conversion suggests nothing of the perseverance needed when the inevitable frustrations inherent in charitable giving surface); and false views of the solutions to social misery (a kind heart and distributed money, not basic changes in either the moral, educational or social structures). Such false – sentimental – views, the objection maintains, encourages audiences to acquire oversimplified beliefs and to act on these oversimplifications.[7]

As a result of having bought into an overly sentimental, Dickensian view of the plight of the poor, we are likely to be misled about its real causes and will not be able to deal effectively with the reality of poverty.

The sentimentality of *A Christmas Carol* could also lead people to permanently lose themselves in this charming escapist fantasy. Ira Newman again:

Sentimentality is conducive to such escapist inclinations because its falsifications involve projecting an appealing quality on its idealized subjects. Thus if the Cratchits and Tiny Tim were presented as seething with resentment, or if Scrooge were not in the end presented as, in Chesterton's words, a 'great furnace of real happiness' – possibilities which would be, no doubt psychologically and socially, more true to life – we would probably not have the degree of fondness for them that we find ourselves so curiously possessing. This suggests the possibility that under some circumstances we might be tempted to remain within the aestheticized sanctuary of the sentimental 'world' itself rather than deal with *real* poor people, whose intractable faults and problems may be the cause of deep discomfort to us.[8]

Joe might perhaps level both these charges at Mary, and with some justification. Doesn't Mary's Christmas round robin involve a potentially very damaging sort of self-deception? Isn't Mary hiding or distorting the truth about their married life together in a way that could, potentially, lead her to act inappropriately? For example, perhaps Mary should have left Joe years ago. Perhaps she has only put up with his awful, priggish behaviour because she has managed to persuade herself of the truth of a ridiculously sentimentalised vision of their married life: the vision presented in her round robins. A marriage can be propped up by kitsch and sentimentality just as effectively as can a totalitarian regime.

## *Genuine Christmas spirit*

Joe has been explaining to Mary how those who indulge in Christmas sentimentality may be less likely to do something about unpleasant reality.

> JOE: So you see: the entire Christmas season is terminally sentimental. The emotions it evokes are self-deceiving. The 'Christmas spirit' is really all about disguising the truth. And that's a dangerous thing.
> MARY: Perhaps I'm guilty of a little self-deception. Maybe, as you say, my round robins do disguise the truth. But your cold-hearted attitude to the spirit of

Christmas certainly isn't justified. Many of the emotions that Christmas evokes are entirely genuine. They needn't involve any sort of self-deception.

JOE: Poppycock. The whole hearty, back-slapping season of 'goodwill' is a sham.

It's easy to slide into cynicism about the kind of emotions that Christmas excites. But while we should, I think, maintain a healthy scepticism, let's not forget that, for all its faults, Christmas has been responsible for some truly inspiring episodes.

Perhaps the most remarkable of all was the spontaneous, unofficial truce that broke out on the front line between English and German soldiers on Christmas Day 1914, and the game of football they played on the frozen no man's land between the trenches. As the German Kurt Zehmisch of the 134th Saxons remembers: 'Eventually the English brought a soccer ball from the trenches, and pretty soon a lively game ensued. How marvelously wonderful, yet how strange it was. The English officers felt the same way about it. Thus Christmas, the celebration of love, managed to bring mortal enemies together as our friends for a time.'[9] True, some might insist that this extraordinary event was in fact a grand exercise in kitsch, that these soldiers were engaged in an escapist fantasy for a day. That strikes me as implausible, however. The suggestion that the Christmas spirit felt by these men towards each other was reality-denying is too much to swallow. The day before, their comrades had been shot to pieces before their very eyes, by the same soldiers with whom they were now exchanging gifts of cake and chocolate. They knew that, on Boxing Day, battle would commence, and that these men would again try to kill them. In some cases, the fraternisation took place while battle raged nearby. On 31 December 1914, Captain Thomas Frost of the 1st Cheshires wrote to his father from the front line about a football match, visits to the German trenches and the exchanging of plum puddings for German sausages. Frost added: 'It seems extraordinary that a desperate fight was going on during this about 800 yards to our left between the French and Germans.'[10] These soldiers clearly weren't pretending that the war did not exist. How could they? Nor were they deluding themselves about how the opposing soldiers felt, for they were in exactly the same situation themselves.

What these men felt towards each other was genuine. It was felt even while they continued to stare the reality of their situation full in the face. In fact, it was felt precisely *because* of their acute awareness of their situation.

The feelings we have at Christmas need not be reality-denying. There is room left for an honest, genuine Christmas spirit. Joe is right in that what passes for the 'spirit of Christmas' is often little more than sentimental kitsch. But Mary is right that it can be much more than that.

---

1 This quote is taken from 'C. S. Lewis on Christmas', an article by Kathryn Lindskoog that appeared in *Christianity Today*, 16 December 1983.

2 C. S. Lewis, 'What Christmas Means to Me', from *God in the Dock – Essays on Theology and Ethics* (London: Fount, 1998).

3 Milan Kundera, *The Unbearable Lightness of Being* (London: Faber, 1984), p. 242.

4 Ibid., p. 242.

5 Ibid., p. 245.

6 Charles Dickens, *A Christmas Carol* (London: Penguin, 1984), p. 15.

7 Ira Newman, 'The Alleged Unwholesomeness of Sentimentality' in Alex Neill and Aaron Ridley (eds), *Arguing About Art*, 2nd edn (London: Routledge, 2002) p. 323.

8 Ibid.

9 Stanley Weintraub, *Silent Night* (London: Simon & Schuster, 2002), p. 119.

10 Ibid., p. 122.

# Peace on Earth

*The Christmas message is one of peace. But what does this mean? Should all Christians embrace pacifism and absolute non-violence? Many (including George Bush and Tony Blair) believe that war can be and sometimes is justified. But can the philosophy of the 'just war' really be reconciled with religious belief?*

At Christmas we wish for 'peace on earth and goodwill to all men'. Jesus is, of course, thought of as a man of peace, and so Christmas is a time for burying the hatchet and loving thy neighbour. The God of the Old Testament, on the other hand, is most certainly a God of war. As Alexander Waugh points out in his book *God*, in the first seven books of the Bible God serves his people, primarily, as a lucky mascot for war. 'He is the Israelites' field marshal. They consult him on tactics and weaponry, giving him dispensation to pick their enemies and decide when, where and how to eliminate them.'[1] God doesn't just condone and direct the Israelites' wars, he sometimes even fights alongside them, and to spectacular effect: throwing hailstones (Josh. 10: 11), calling the stars to action (Judg. 5: 20) and preventing the sun from setting to give the Israelites more time to smash their enemies (Josh. 10: 12).

God's tactics were not always successful. In one action, when the Israelites asked his advice on which tribe should go first into battle, God told them it should be Judah. 'The Judean regiments dutifully marched forward and 22,000 men were massacred. Wiping tears from their eyes, the other soldiers went back to God and asked him, "Are you really sure we should continue this battle?" "March against them!" God ordered . . . Once again they were defeated and 18,000 of them met their deaths.'[2]

Not only were God's battle-orders sometimes fairly unorthodox, they could also be merciless. God took no prisoners, demanding the execution of men, women and children. The Bible tells us, for example, that 'So Joshua smote all the country, and . . . left none remaining, but utterly destroyed all that breathed, as the Lord God of Israel commanded' (Josh. 10: 40). Peace, in short, does not appear to be a particularly high priority for the God portrayed in the Old Testament.

When we turn to the New Testament and the teachings of Jesus, we find Old Testament attitudes to war and violence apparently turned on their head. In Romans, Paul says: 'Bless them which persecute you . . . Recompense to no man evil for evil . . . Be not overcome by evil, but overcome evil by good' (Rom. 12: 14, 17, 21). Jesus himself says: 'Blessed are the peacemakers, for they shall be called the children of God' (Matt. 5: 9). And, perhaps most famously of all, Jesus instructs us to 'turn the other cheek': 'But I say unto you, that ye resist not evil: but whosoever shall smite thee on thy right cheek, turn to him the other one also.' (Matt. 5: 39).

As a result of Jesus's teaching, for the next 250 years many Christians eschewed all forms of violence. As a consequence, some went like lambs to the slaughter. They even showed no resistance when thrown to the lions for public entertainment.

## *Absolute non-violence*

This sort of absolute non-violence and pacifism still appeals to some. One of its attractions is that it merely extends to wider conflicts what many of us think about killing outside war – that it is absolutely prohibited. The fact that the killing should be performed by a man in a uniform on the instruction of his government rather than by a man with a stocking over his head on the instruction of an accomplice seems, to some, to be entirely irrelevant to its moral character.

But, of course, the vast majority of us believe that a resort to violence and even killing, at least in times of war, is sometimes the lesser of two evils. In fact, the position of absolute non-violence has been accused of logical incoherence.

For example, the philosopher Jan Narveson[3] argues that if we say that violence is always morally wrong, then we contradict ourselves. For to preach non-violence is to take the view that those who are the victims of violence have a right not to have violence inflicted on them. But having such a right also involves the right to take whatever action might be necessary (other things being equal) to prevent those rights being infringed. But violence itself might be necessary to prevent violence being done. So could an absolute prohibition on violence give us the right to use it?

The philosopher Jonathan Glover deals with this

particular criticism of absolute non-violence by pointing out, correctly, that Narveson simply assumes that if violence is wrong, then we have the right to use *any* means necessary to protect ourselves. But that simply doesn't follow. 'To think that something is wrong, is not to think that the victims have a no-holds-barred right of self-defence.'[4] So there is nothing incoherent about the position of absolute non-violence. That's not to say, however, that it is the right position to adopt.

Some seem to think that embracing absolute non-violence is the right thing to do because it will lead, in the long run, to greater happiness and contentment all round. When Paul says, for example, 'Be not overcome by evil, but overcome evil with good', the suggestion seems to be, not just that we shouldn't resort to violence, but that by refusing it and by doing good instead, we will, with God's help, actually succeed in overcoming the evil pitted against us. The non-violent will ultimately triumph.

There may be some truth in this. If we repeatedly turn the other cheek, the person striking us may begin to question what he or she is doing, and eventually cease. Non-violent resistance movements have certainly suc-ceeded where more aggressive strategies have failed. Gandhi's peaceful methods did, ultimately, remove the British from India and Martin Luther King's non-violent resistance to racial segregation also achieved its aim. Both Gandhi's and King's pacificism increased the shame felt by their oppressors, making the latter's position seem even more morally untenable.

On the other hand, there are plenty of oppressors who are entirely unmoved by non-violent resistance. Turn the other cheek and they will take the opportunity to strike that too. With something large and spiky. The evidence strongly suggests that those who suppose otherwise have a rather unrealistic view of human nature.

In fact, it seems probable that, by publicly adopting a non-violent position, you are actually likely to encourage others to attack you, for they know they will get away with it. The non-violence of Tibetan Buddhists certainly appears to have done little to diminish the viciousness of the treatment handed out to them by the Chinese.

Worse still, the aggression you encourage may not affect you alone. When someone discovers that you have turned the other cheek and capitulated when they have struck you or cheated you, they may well extend their aggression and cheating to others. For, as the philosopher Peter Singer points out, you have just taught them that aggression and cheating pay. True, we generally hold in high regard those who turn the other cheek. 'Most of us think that turning the other cheek is a noble ideal, even if too idealistic for this world . . . Consequently we admire those who are prepared to act on it. If they are prepared to be struck on both cheeks, we think, they are the *only* ones who are likely to be worse off.'[5] But does cheek-turning seem quite so admirable once we understand that the unpleasant consequences are likely to affect not just the cheek-turner, but the rest of us too? 'To turn the other cheek is to teach would-be cheats that cheating pays. There is not much attraction in an ethic of turning the other cheek if the resulting hardship falls not only on those who allow themselves to be struck, but on everyone else as a whole.'[6]

So embrace absolute non-violence if you like. It may even be the right thing to do. But it seems unwise to embrace it because you think it will ultimately – in perhaps one hundred or even one thousand years – lead to the triumph of good over evil. Nine times out of ten, if non-violence is the right thing to practise, it's going to have to be the right thing *despite* the outcome, which is often very nasty and brutal indeed. And the consequence of embracing non-violence is likely to be not just your own misery, but also that of the next victim down the line.

That turning the other cheek really is too idealistic for this world is certainly what the majority of Christians now believe, which is why they are willing to condone the 'just war'.

## *The just war*

Whilst Jesus is a man of peace, the extent to which Christians are committed to it has varied enormously down through the centuries. For about 250 years after Christ, violence of any sort was held by many to be against Jesus's teaching, though the extent to which the early Christians were actually pacifist is controversial. Certainly, a number refused to join the military – but whether this was because they were pacifists or because they disliked the pagan religious cult that was widespread in the army is not entirely clear. In later centuries, of course, Christian enthusiasm for war increased, and during the Crusades battle was regularly waged in God's name.

Augustine, one of the early Church fathers, is also one

of the most important Christian thinkers on war. Augustine argued that Christians could, in good conscience, serve in the Roman military and wage war if two conditions were met.

First, the war had to be waged by a legitimate authority (in Rome, in Augustine's day, this would have been the Emperor, who, it was supposed, was appointed by God). Second, there had to be a just cause: a state could not go to war simply to further its own expansionist aims. It had to be correcting a real injustice.

These conditions for a just war were later refined by other religious thinkers. In the twelfth century, St Thomas Aquinas emphasised the importance of a third condition: that war should be fought with a good intention. Aquinas noted that the first two conditions could be met in a war waged by aggressors who, while they might happen to have justice on their side, were nevertheless really pursuing the war for all the wrong reasons: perhaps out of revenge or a desire to expand their empire. Aquinas insisted that those waging war must do it for the right reasons. (Incidentally, although Aquinas is often credited with adding this third condition, it appears that Augustine had already included it as Aquinas cites Augustine as his authority.)[7]

In the sixteenth century the Spanish moralist Francisco Vittoria added a fourth condition: that war should be fought by proper means. It is wrong, argued Vittoria, to target innocent civilians and use disproportionate force. In 1983 the Catholic bishops of America further refined the conditions. Like Vittoria, they also carefully distinguished between the question of when it is right to go to war and how war should be fought. The bishops suggested that the conditions governing *when* it is right to go to war are:

1. There must be a just cause.
2. War must be declared by a competent and legal authority.
3. Comparative justice: the claims of those in whose name war is waged must significantly outweigh those against whom the war is waged.
4. There must be a right intention.
5. War must be the last resort.
6. War must be likely to succeed.
7. The death and suffering that the war causes must be significantly outweighed by the need to correct the injustice over which the war is fought.

The conditions governing *how* war should be waged are:

8. Proportionality: we must not resort to nuclear weapons to solve some minor border dispute.
9. Noncombatant immunity: civilians should not be deliberately targeted.
10. Right intention: strikes should be made not out of vengeance and anger, but should be performed with the aim of peace and justice in mind.

Some of these conditions might, perhaps, be questioned. During the Second World War the Allies, in effect, rejected the ninth; the bombing of German civilians was justified on the grounds that no one is a noncombatant as everyone is contributing in some way to the war effort. But if war is to be waged at all, it does seem plausible that most, if not all, of these conditions should be satisfied. The devil, of course, is in the detail. When faced with an actual dispute, it is usually highly debatable whether or not the conditions have been adequately met. As I write, US and UK military forces have just 'liberated' Iraq after severe bombing campaigns across the nation. Was this military action just?

Many say no. The war was not fought by the relevant legal authority – the UN – but by the US and UK going it alone, and in spite of enormous protests from ordinary civilians. It was also fought for all the wrong reasons: to increase US strategic control over the Middle East, especially over its oil reserves, and in revenge against the Arab world for 9/11 (despite the fact that there is no evidence of any Iraqi involvement in 9/11). Nor was this a war of last resort: the sanctions previously applied against Iraq to force it to disarm were seen to be working.

Yet many Christians insisted that this war was just, Tony Blair and George Bush included. They said that the intention was good: that it was a 'moral' war to remove Iraq's weapons of mass destruction and to free the people from a tyrannical regime. They also insisted that it was a war of last resort: all other avenues for getting Saddam Hussein to disarm had been exhausted. And the US and UK were entirely appropriate authorities to wage this war: they are democratic nation states, after all.

Real wars are complex and, in most cases, a fairly plausible-looking argument can be put up both for the view that the war is 'just' and also for condemning it. The Catholic bishops' conditions are helpful, but in reality they rarely ever settle the question of whether or not we should go to war.

## *Self-defence and weapons*

While St Augustine insisted that war might be justly fought, he was less enthusiastic about individual Christians killing privately in their own defence. However, many Christians now happily carry and are prepared to use guns, particularly in the US.

So how do gun-carrying Christians who are willing to shoot in self-defence reconcile their attitude with Jesus's injunction to turn the other cheek? At www.keepandbear-arms.com, one of the many websites dedicated to justifying gun ownership, Pastor Roger Margerison presents 'Turn the Other Cheek – Clarified' in which he helpfully explains what Jesus really meant. 'The statement of Jesus to turn the other cheek is simply this, "Slap me because of my testimony for Christ or because I have done you wrong and I will turn the other cheek (or try to). Slap me because I am ugly and I will slap you back." '[8]

This is a fairly typical reading of Jesus among the gun-toting public. Christians like Pastor Margerison are also fond of pointing out that while Jesus did indeed tell Peter to put away his sword, he did not instruct him to get rid of it altogether. 'People have a terminal misconception about what the Bible says about gun control. Peter did not carry a Glock or Uzi but he did carry a sword. Jesus was told by a disciple on the way to the Garden that they had two swords. He did not tell them to take them off.'[9]

Despite what Christ's early followers apparently took his words to mean, modern interpreters like Pastor Margerison are confident they know better. If you are faced with an intruder menacing you in your home, letting rip with your semi-automatic is apparently fine by Him.

1 Alexander Waugh, *God* (London: Headline, 2002), p. 226.
2 Ibid., pp. 226–7.
3 Jan Narveson, 'Pacifism: A Philosophical Analysis', *Ethics*, 1965.
4 Jonathan Glover, *Causing Death and Saving Lives* (London: Pelican, 1977), p. 257.
5 Peter Singer, *How Are We to Live?* (Oxford: Oxford University Press, 1996), p. 164.
6 Ibid.
7 St Thomas Aquinas, *Summa Theologica*, vol. II, Chapter 2, question 40.1.
8 Roger Margerison, www.keepandbeararms.com/information
9 Ibid.

# 6

## The Incarnation

*Are we, at Christmas, celebrating the birth of an entity as contradictory as a round square?*

Christmas is a celebration of the incarnation. Jesus of Nazareth is supposed to be God incarnate: both God and man. That might seem a fairly straightforward sort of claim. People may argue over whether it is true, of course, but that what is being claimed is clear and coherent is largely taken for granted on both sides. Which is odd, because the dispute over exactly how divinity and humanity are combined in the person of Jesus is one of the deepest and most ill-tempered in Christian history. Philosophers and theologians have been struggling to make sense of the incarnation for over two thousand years. The early Church fathers fought bitterly over the issue and it remains a source of contention to this day.

So what, exactly, is the difficulty? Here's an analogy. Suppose I tell you that I have drawn a circle on a sheet of paper. I then tell you that not only is it a circle, but also a square. How would you respond? With great bewilderment, I imagine. To claim that my circle is also a square is *not* like claiming that, say, Charles Dickens was also Prime Minister of England, because even though the latter statement is false, we can at least make sense of the suggestion that it might be true. The claim may be false, but at least it's coherent. When it comes to the suggestion that my circle is also a square, what I claim is not so much false as nonsensical.

There are certain properties that something must possess if it is to be a circle, which it cannot possess if it is also a square. A circle, by definition, cannot have any straight sides. A square, on the other hand, must have straight sides. Therefore nothing can be both a circle and a square on pain of contradiction. That is why you know that there can be no square circles. You don't need to look to see whether I have succeeded in drawing a square circle. You already know, just by thinking it through, that my claim cannot be true.

The same, some argue, is true of the idea that Jesus is both God and man. The claim that such a being exists also involves a contradiction. So again, just by thinking about it, we can determine that no such person exists. We don't even need to look at the historical evidence.

But what is contradictory about the idea of the incarnation? Many things, it seems. Here are three examples.

To begin with, let's remind ourselves of a few of God's properties. God is of course omnipotent and omniscient: all-powerful and all-knowing. There is nothing God cannot do; nor is there anything he does not know. God is also eternal: he was not created and he is not the kind of being that can die. All of these properties possessed by God are essential properties. A being that lacked any one of them would not be God.

But now what of Jesus, the man? Jesus, as a human being, had only a limited sort of knowledge. The Bible says that he grew in wisdom (Luke 2: 52), which implies that at one time he knew less than he did later. And Jesus himself admitted that there were things he did not know, such as the time when heaven and earth would pass away (Mark 13: 32). So we have discovered a property – omniscience that God has to possess, but that Jesus, if scripture is to be believed, lacked. We are therefore in a position to argue as follows:

God is omniscient.
Jesus is not omniscient.
Therefore Jesus is not God.

Here is a second apparent contradiction generated by the doctrine of incarnation. We know that Jesus had certain weaknesses. He was subject to temptation, for example. But God, being omnipotent, has no weaknesses and is beyond temptation. So the following argument holds:

God is omnipotent.
Jesus is not omnipotent.
Therefore Jesus is not God.

Third, we know that Jesus died – this is an essential part of Christian belief. But God necessarily cannot die. So, again, it follows that Jesus is not God:

God cannot die.
Jesus died.
Therefore Jesus is not God.

These three arguments are just examples. Many other contradictions also appear to be generated by the suggestion that Jesus was both God and man.

## *How to prove that things are not identical*

The three arguments presented above all make use of a very famous logical principle called Leibniz's law (after the philosopher Leibniz, who formulated it). Leibniz's law says that if two things are identical – if they are one and the same entity – then whatever properties one has, the other should have, and vice versa. So, for example, if John Wayne is one and the same person as Marion Morrison (which he was: 'John Wayne' was the actor's stage name), then any property possessed by John Wayne must be possessed by Marion Morrison. If John Wayne is six foot three, then so is Marion Morrison. If John Wayne rode a horse, then so did Marion Morrison. If John Wayne could throw a mean punch, then so could Marion Morrison.

Leibniz's law comes in handy if you want to test whether two things that might appear to be one and the same thing really are identical. Suppose, for example, that a friend tells you that they recently met someone called 'John Smith' at the supermarket. You also happen to know someone by that name, but of course it's a common name, so you wonder whether it really could be the same John Smith that you know. How might you test the claim that they are the same person?

One way would be to see if the properties of the supermarket John Smith match those of your John Smith. Does he have dark hair? Is he tall? Does he speak with a

Northern accent? If you can find a property that one John Smith possesses that the other does not, then it follows, by Leibniz's law, that they're not one and the same.

Notice that the three arguments outlined above that appear to show that Jesus is not God all rely on this form of reasoning. Each points out that God has a property that Jesus lacks, and then concludes that Jesus cannot be God. The doctrine of the incarnation runs up against Leibniz's law.

## *The Council of Chalcedon*

The debate over Christ's divinity raged heatedly for several centuries after his death. Some early Christians, such as Apollinaris, insisted that Jesus was not a human being at all. Jesus took on a human body, but he did not become a human, for he did not possess a human soul. So while Jesus might appear to have had various human characteristics incompatible with also being divine, that appearance was illusory.

Apollinaris's view neatly solves the puzzle of how Jesus could be both human and divine. He merely seemed human. But most Christians have been unable to accept this solution to the puzzle. For them, it is essential that Jesus be both fully God and fully man. His full humanity and solidarity with the human race are usually held to be essential if Jesus is to be our redeemer.

Others – the Nestorians – insisted that Jesus was, in effect, two individuals: one human and one divine. That, again, would remove the appearance of contradiction. But

here too, most Christians find the two-individuals suggestion rather repellent, in part because it again raises
seemingly impossible obstacles to redemption.

As I say, the debate raged for centuries, often descend-
ing into acrimony, until finally, in AD 451, the various
warring churches met at Chalcedon and agreed on a
common position. The Council of Chalcedon decreed
that Jesus had two natures: he was both truly human and
truly divine. But these two natures had come together and
were both preserved within a single person. The Chalce-
donian council rejected both the Nestorian view that Jesus
was not a single person, and also the Apollinarian position
that Jesus was not fully human.

## Is Jesus's divinity merely metaphorical?

Of course, the Council of Chalcedon's definition con-
fronts us with precisely the problem with which we
started: that of explaining how Jesus's two natures –
human and divine – could possibly be reconciled, without
contradiction, in a single person.

Some contemporary Christians, including John Hick
(whose analogy of the square circle I have borrowed),
have argued that Chalcedon simply got it wrong. The
Chalcedon doctrine of two natures combined within a
single individual is a confused attempt to make literal sense
of what should be understood metaphorically. Jesus was
not, literally, God. He was God 'incarnate' only in a
metaphorical sense, that is to say, only in the sense that he
was a 'human being extraordinarily open to God's
influence and thus living to an extraordinary extent as

God's agent on earth, "incarnating" the divine purpose for human life'.[1] There have been a great many religious figures that have 'incarnated' God's purpose in this way, so they are *all* God 'incarnate'. There is, in this respect, nothing exceptional about Jesus – he was just another important holy man.

This modern take on the incarnation is obviously unorthodox, and does not fit entirely comfortably with scripture, which repeatedly states, quite unambiguously, that Jesus was God.

## *Jesus's 'two minds'*

Others believe Chalcedon can be salvaged. The philosopher Richard Swinburne provides a rather ingenious explanation of Jesus's apparent ignorance by maintaining, not the Nestorian position that there are, in effect, two individuals in Christ (which, as we saw above, would be contrary to Chalcedon), but that he was a single individual possessing two minds.[2]

Swinburne points out that, post-Freud, we now have a better understanding of how a single person can possess a divided mind. A mother, for example, might consciously believe that her son is alive, and yet unconsciously know that he is dead. When she is asked whether her son is still alive, she will answer, quite sincerely, 'Yes.' Yet in another, unconscious part of her mind she clearly accepts his death – which is indicated by the fact that she throws his possessions away. A belief can happily exist in one part of someone's mind without being accessible to another part of it.

Similarly, explains Swinburne, we can suppose that Jesus's mind was divided. His divine mind was omniscient and knew everything, but within this divine, all-knowing consciousness resided a human consciousness that was partitioned off from the rest. Jesus's human mind could not access the rest of his larger, divine mind. That is why, despite the fact that Jesus was God, and thus omniscient, his human mind could be ignorant of various things, and could grow in wisdom.

## *A puzzle*

At Christmas, Christians celebrate the incarnation, an extremely mystifying event. Indeed, the doctrine of the incarnation seems, on the face of it, not to make much sense. While philosophers and theologians have striven to explain how full humanity and full divinity can be combined within a single person, the incarnation remains, for many, a deep and seemingly intractable puzzle.

---

1 John Hick, *The Metaphor of God Incarnate: Christology in a Pluralistic Age* (Louisville: Cambridge University Press, 1993), p. 12.
2 Richard Swinburne, *The Christian God* (Oxford: Oxford University Press, 1994), Chapter 9.

# 7

## Santa Claus, Coke and the 'Commercial Racket'

*Christmas, we are all aware, is becoming ever more commercial. But what, exactly, is wrong with that? Why not whip out the credit card and go on a spree . . . ?*

We think of Santa Claus as an ancient, highly traditional figure. In our minds, his image has acquired the patina of centuries of tradition. But in actual fact, Santa's current appearance is in large part down to the Coca-Cola company.

In the 1930s Coca-Cola commissioned illustrator Haddon H. Sundblom to produce a series of illustrations portraying Santa Claus. Instead of the traditional pipe, Sundblom made Santa hold a Coke. And while Santa had previously been portrayed in red and white (although not exclusively so: he was also fond of green costumes), it was Sundblom who designed his natty red and white two-piece suit with the big belt, the floppy boots and matching hat. Red and white are, of course, the company's colours. So the 'traditional' image we have of Santa is in large part a product of a highly successful advertising campaign. What seems age-old actually originated in a twentieth-century company boardroom.

For those already cynical about the commercialisation of Christmas, this discovery about Santa will merely confirm their attitude. 'See?' they'll say. 'What looks like an innocent, traditional celebration of the birth of Christ has been hijacked by commerce. Christmas is now almost entirely about *selling more stuff*: more Coke, more cards, more food, more useless plastic tat.'

Christmas is certainly big business. The plastic Santas start to make an appearance in store windows as early as October, and sales soon begin to climb. The news immediately after Christmas is often dominated by reports about how well business did over the Christmas period. If the figures are not as good as was hoped, a gloom can settle over the country. So Christmas clearly matters to the economy.

But is that such a bad thing? Before we start lamenting how commercial Christmas has become, let's not forget that, by stimulating the economy, Christmas generates wealth and creates jobs. And that's to be welcomed, surely? Aren't those who insist we rein in our Christmas spending spree asking us, in effect, to cripple the economy and put people out of work?

## C. S. Lewis on the 'commercial racket'

In 1957 C. S. Lewis published 'What Christmas Means to Me'. As mentioned in Chapter 4, Lewis points out that three things go by the name of 'Christmas': a religious festival, a holiday and a 'commercial racket'. The 'racket' he condemns on four grounds.

First, the whole business gives us far more pain than pleasure:

You have only to stay over Christmas with a family who seriously try to 'keep' it (in its third, or commercial, aspect) in order to see that the thing is a nightmare . . . They look far more as if there had been a long illness in the house.

Second, it is involuntary:

The modern rule is that anyone can force you to give him a present by sending you a quite unprovoked present of his own. It is almost a blackmail.

Third, the presents are often things which 'no mortal ever bought for himself – gaudy and useless gadgets, "novelties" because no one was ever fool enough to make their like before.'

And, finally, there's the awful nuisance the Christmas racket causes:

We are told that the whole dreary business must go on because it is good for trade. It in in fact merely one annual symptom of that lunatic condition of our country, and indeed of the world, in which everyone lives by persuading everyone else to buy things. I don't know the way out. But can it really be my duty to buy and receive masses of junk every winter just to help the shopkeepers?[1]

A good question. Indeed, is the endless economic growth, to which Christmas is in large part designed to contribute, necessarily a good thing? Or even sustainable?

## *Consumerism and happiness*

Christmas should, perhaps, remind us that there is more to life than simply accumulating wealth and possessions. Many of us tend to operate with what might be called a consumerist model of happiness: that is, we tend to think of the good life in terms of the acquisition of more and more stuff – more wealth, bigger houses, more gadgets, flashier cars.

At Christmas, of course, we're particularly keen to acquire such things. And we give and receive more material possessions than at any other time of the year. Children expect literally sack-loads of new toys. But does this increase in material abundance actually make us any happier?

We Westerners have become significantly wealthier over the last few decades. We own more colour TVs, more video recorders, more DVD players, more micro-waves and more cars than ever before. And yet it seems we are not appreciably happier. The University of Chicago's National Opinion Research Center regularly polls Americans to find out how happy they feel. The proportion describing themselves as 'very happy' has remained about one third since the 1950s, despite the fact that people have become far more affluent. Indeed, people don't perceive themselves to be more affluent, despite the fact that they are. Why so?

Some argue that the explanation lies in a feature of human psychology known as adaptation. Here, for example, is Paul Wachtel:

★

In judging how well off we are economically . . . we assimilate new input to our 'adaptation level'. For many Americans, having one or several color television sets, two or more cars, a home in which there are more rooms than people . . . these and other features of their lives are experienced as the 'neutral point'. They do not excite us or arouse much feeling. Only a departure from that level is really noticed. Some pleasure may be afforded by our background level of material comfort, but unless we look elsewhere than the accumulation of goods for the main sources of pleasure and excitement in our lives, we are bound to be on a treadmill – one which, we are increasingly recognizing, can damage our health and shorten our lives.[2]

As a result of adaptation, we have become accustomed to rising levels of affluence. When affluence continues to increase, but at a slower rate, people actually end up feeling less happy and perceive themselves to be poorer than they were before. The endless spiral of material acquisition cannot in fact make us more content. Like a drug addict, we simply become accustomed to whatever we're getting, cease to derive much pleasure from it, and so start demanding even more. As a result, explains the philosopher Peter Singer, 'once we have satisfied our basic needs, there is no level of material comfort at which we are likely to find significantly greater long-term fulfillment than any other level.'[3]

And of course, ever-rising levels of consumption are impossible to maintain, for the resources on which we are drawing are finite. Not only are we damaging ourselves in pursuing our addiction to acquisitive materialism, we are also damaging the environment, eventually to the point where it will be beyond repair. Singer argues that we need fundamentally to rethink our attitudes to contentment, and to reject the consumerist model of happiness that is dragging us all to our doom. Perhaps Christmas, the great annual festival of consumerism, would be a good place to start.

---

1 C. S. Lewis, 'What Christmas Means to Me' from *God in the Dock – Essays on Theology and Ethics* (London: Fount, 1998).

2 Paul Wachtel, *The Poverty of Affluence* (New York: Free Press, 1983), p. 60. Also quoted in Peter Singer, *How Are We to Live?* (Oxford, Oxford University Press, 1996).

3 Singer, op.cit., p. 61.

# The Nativity
# and Other Miracles

*Is it reasonable to believe that Mary conceived a child directly from God? Indeed, what evidence is there to believe that religious miracles happen at all? The eighteenth-century philosopher David Hume famously argued that it is unreasonable to believe that any miracle has occurred.*

## The Christmas miracle

At the very heart of Christmas we find a miracle: a virgin birth. Christians believe that their saviour was both conceived and born of a virgin: Mary. But how reasonable is it to suppose that this miracle really took place?

The key witnesses concerning the virgin birth are of course Mary and Joseph, her husband, who is supposed to have seen an angel. This angel explained that Mary would bear a child while she was still a virgin, and that the child would be the son of God (according to the Gospel of Matthew, that is; Luke has the angel appear to Mary herself, while neither John nor Mark makes any mention of a virgin birth).

Now, suppose that the unmarried couple living down the street from you made the same claim. Mary, who lives at number 23, declares that she has conceived a child while still a virgin. Her partner, Joseph, explains over the garden fence that an angel confirmed to him that Mary's child was the result of divine intervention. No doubt both you and your neighbours would be extremely suspicious, not to say amused. Perhaps someone had sex with, or somehow managed to impregnate, Mary while she was sleeping (her partner, for example, who then made up the 'angel' story to cover his tracks). Or perhaps Mary had sex with someone else and then lied to Joseph about her 'immaculate conception'. Maybe one or both of them are mad. Or they may simply be lying, perhaps because they enjoy being the centre of attention and want to sell their story to the tabloids. These are all possibilities that, I imagine, you wouldn't entirely discount. In fact, my guess is that you would consider the suggestion that Mary really *had* conceived a child directly from God as one of the least plausible explanations of what was going on.

So why should we take the Biblical Mary and Joseph's word for it? Particularly as we cannot talk to them directly, but have to rely on second- or even third-hand testimony? The eighteenth-century philosopher Thomas Paine expressed just such doubts:

> When I am told that a woman called the Virgin Mary, said, or gave out, that she was with child without any cohabitation with man, and that her betrothed husband, Joseph, said that an angel told him so, I have a right to believe them or not; such a circumstance requires a much stronger evidence than their bare word for it; but we have not even this – for neither Joseph nor Mary wrote any such matter themselves; it is only reported by

others that they said so – it is hearsay upon hearsay, and I do not choose to rest my belief upon such evidence.[1]

But is this piecemeal approach to assessing the evidence entirely right? Isn't there a great deal of evidence that Jesus was a miraculous being of miraculous origin? For example, unlike the 'virgin birth' down the street, the Biblical one was apparently prophesied, in Isaiah 7: 14.

The claim that Jesus was born of a virgin fits coherently with a much wider web of religious belief and there are many other miracles associated with Jesus's life. He is reported to have raised Lazarus from the dead, turned water into wine and made the blind see. Also Jesus was himself supposedly resurrected after death. All these miracles were witnessed by many people, none of whom we have any particular reason to distrust.

So while the evidence provided by Mary's and Joseph's testimony (or rather, the testimony about what their testimony was), when considered in isolation, might fall short of the standards required for sensible belief, perhaps a cumulative case might be made. Perhaps the evidence, taken as a whole, rationally supports belief in Jesus's divine origin?

## Other religious miracles

The Old Testament is a rich source of stories about seemingly miraculous events. It includes a detailed account of how God parted the Red Sea in order to allow the Israelites to escape from their Egyptian pursuers, an event that was supposedly witnessed by a huge number of people. Doesn't their collective testimony give us good grounds to suppose that this miracle really happened? The Old Testament also describes many other dramatic miracles, from the destruction of cities to the conjuring up of pillars of fire and the turning of human beings into salt. Again, all of these miracles were witnessed by many people.

If the Bible is to be believed, this was a period in which God was very active, creating all sorts of highly spectacular events. But what of today? Woody Allen once asked, 'My Lord! My Lord! What hast Thou done lately?'[2] Perhaps that's a little unfair. God may not recently have done anything quite as spectacular as parting a sea, but many believe he is still highly active, intervening in all sorts of ways.

That is certainly what many Catholics believe. In order for someone to be canonised as a saint within the Catholic faith, two things are required. First, there must be good evidence that the person in question had great virtues – virtues in a 'heroic degree'. Second, the candidate must have performed at least two miracles – posthumously. After the death of Mother Teresa, for example, many prayed to her asking for her intervention and there have been several reports of miracles performed in response to those prayers. These claims are being investigated by the relevant papal authorities to see if the miracles are genuine and, if they are, Mother Teresa may yet be canonised.

Since the present Pope was ordained in 1978, 464 saints have been canonised. That means that at least 928 miracles have been verified. So, according to the Catholic Church, God continues to make a great many miracles happen.

Protestants also regularly report the occurrence of miracles. Many are alleged to have taken place during

Evangelical services, with one reported case of amalgam fillings turning to gold in people's mouths.[3]

In short, reports of miracles continue apace, not only in the Christian world but in many other faiths too. How credible are these reports? How reasonable is it to suppose that any of these miracles has really ever occurred.

## *Two sorts of 'miracle'*

Before we begin to assess the evidence, let's clarify exactly what we mean by a 'miracle'. What is required in order for an event to qualify as genuinely miraculous?

For most religious believers, any genuine miracle requires that a divine power somehow intervenes in the natural order to bring about an event that would not otherwise have occurred. God makes something happen that is actually contrary to the laws of nature. I call miracles of this sort supernatural miracles, because they involve the intervention of a supernatural agency. But does a miracle necessarily have to involve divine intervention and the suspension of natural law?

The philosopher R. F. Holland suggests not. He asks us to imagine the following situation: a child has become trapped on a railway line and is about to be run over and killed by a train. But then something fantastically unlikely happens: a sequence of chance events – the driver happens to pass out, releasing the drive handle – causes the train to stop just in time. Here, an entirely natural series of incidents results in the saving of the child without an external power having to intervene and change what is happening. Yet, as Holland points out, most of us would call what happened a 'miracle'. The event is a 'miracle' in the sense that it is an extremely fortuitous coincidence. And of course, we can all agree that such happy coincidences happen. So we can also agree that, in a sense, 'miracles happen'. This is a perfectly familiar and proper use of the term.[4]

This is not, however, what most religious people usually mean when they speak of miracles. Still, some might suggest that while the case Holland describes might not involve a supernatural miracle, it might still constitute an example of 'divine providence'. Perhaps God did act to save the child, but without his having to suspend the laws of nature. Perhaps God, at the moment of creation, looked into the future and saw that the child would become trapped, and so he set in motion a series of events that would inevitably give rise to the child being saved. God deliberately saved the child, but did so by working through the laws of nature, not against them.

## *Happy coincidences and divine intervention*

Many, when presented with a 'miracle' of the sort Holland describes, would think it implausible that such a fortuitous and unlikely event should happen just by chance. That the train driver should pass out at exactly *that* moment, so saving the child, just by chance, is surely too much to swallow. Surely, they would say, isn't it far more plausible that God *was* somehow involved? Wouldn't this be the reasonable thing to believe?

I think not. We should actually expect reports, entirely accurate reports, of astonishing happy coincidences from time to time, whether or not God exists. In fact, the existence of such coincidences is overwhelmingly probable. Just think of the odds of any particular person holding a single winning lottery ticket. The probability is tiny – in the UK it is in the region of 14 million to one against – so, for the person who wins, their win is a miracle in the sense that it is a fantastically unlikely and fortuitous coincidence. But, of course, there is no justification for supposing that their win is anything other than a result of chance. There is not the slightest reason to believe that someone must have secretly rigged the lottery in this person's favour. For clearly *someone* had to win the lottery, and whoever won would have been no less unlikely to win. A highly improbable event was, in one way, inevitable.

Similarly, as billions of us go through the lottery of life, some are bound to get very lucky indeed. We should expect thousands to experience amazingly happy coincidences. We should expect a handful to be the recipients of absolutely awesome, mind-boggling good luck. Highly unusual chains of cause and effect, such as the scenario Holland imagines involving the child and the train, are to be expected. Indeed, what would be truly astonishing is if such fortuitous coincidences didn't occur on a fairly regular basis.

Those who are tempted to put such events down to divine intervention or providence should also remember that for every train that is halted just before disaster strikes, another is disastrously re-routed right into a crowd of people. There are as many unhappy coincidences as there are happy ones. Are we to suppose, then, that God sometimes acts to make these bad things happen? Presumably not. But then why suppose he is responsible for happy coincidences?

## *The Red Sea miracle*

Occasionally, what might appear to be a supernatural miracle, what may look like a violation of natural law, can turn out to have a perfectly natural explanation.

Take, for example, the Old Testament story of the parting of the Red Sea. The Bible says that, when the Israelites were fleeing the Egyptians, their path was blocked by the sea. It seemed all was lost, but then 'the Lord caused the sea to go back by a strong east wind all the night, and made the sea dry land, and the waters were divided' (Exod. 14: 21). This movement of the sea allowed the Israelites to escape. God then let the water flow back, drowning the Israelites' pursuers. Surely, you might think, if the Red Sea really did move in that way, it could only be because God directly intervened.

However, recently, two oceanographers have explained that, because of the Red Sea's underlying structure, a strong wind can quite naturally result in the water moving to produce dry land. They write:

[Suppose] a uniform wind is allowed to blow over the entire gulf for a period of about a day . . . It is shown, in a similar fashion to the familiar wind setup in a long and narrow lake, the water at the edge of the gulf slowly recedes away from its original prewind position . . . It is found that, even for moderate storms . . . a receding distance of more than one kilometer and a sea level drop of more than 2.5 meters are obtained.[5]

The movement of the Red Sea is usually thought of as a spectacular event like that represented in Cecil B. De Mille's 1956 film *The Ten Commandments*, in which Moses (played by Charlton Heston) leads the Israelites between two towering walls of water. But perhaps what really happened was that the wind blew and the waters shifted in the way that the oceanographers describe. After all, the Biblical text supports the suggestion that the waters were moved by 'a strong wind'. It may be that the Red Sea event never happened. But if it did, then perhaps these oceanographers are correct and no divine intervention is required to explain it. What occurred would still qualify as a 'miracle' in the sense that it was a fantastically fortuitous coincidence (or, at least, fortuitous for the Israelites; not quite so lucky for the Egyptians).

Of course, the 'miracle' might still be seen as an example of divine providence. Perhaps God, knowing that the Israelites would otherwise be slaughtered by the Egyptians, created a universe within which the sea would quite naturally shift at precisely the required moment.

## A naturalistic explanation of the virgin birth?

Having distinguished two different sorts of miracle – supernatural interventions versus fortuitous coincidences – what of Jesus's birth? What sort of miracle are we talking about here?

Would a virgin birth *necessarily* require divine intervention? Perhaps not. Some simpler organisms such as insects can reproduce quite spontaneously without any sexual activity. The process is called parthenogenesis. Parthenogenesis has also been observed in the eggs of mammals, such as rabbits, although only after the eggs have been exposed to unusual combinations of temperature and chemicals. There are no well-documented cases of parthenogenesis occurring naturally in mammals, and certainly not in humans. Still, we cannot be absolutely sure that it is totally impossible in humans. Perhaps a virgin birth is not entirely contrary to the laws of nature. Perhaps it is just extremely improbable.

This is not, of course, how Christians typically view the birth of Christ. For Christians, the conception of Jesus within the womb of Mary was a result of the activity of the Holy Ghost. We should also remember that Christmas marks two things: both the miracle of the virgin birth and the incarnation. Clearly, the incarnation involves the supernatural. Indeed, it requires not just that God, a supernatural being, intervene in the natural realm, but that he should make an appearance within it.

## *Do supernatural miracles happen?*

A great deal of the evidence for miracles takes the form of testimony. There is the testimony of the authors of the Bible (who, in some cases, are already relying on the testimony of others). Most of the evidence for contemporary miracles also consists of reports of what people claim to have witnessed. How much trust should we place in what other people say?

The best-known philosophical discussion of miracles is to be found in the eighteenth-century philosopher David Hume's *Enquiry Concerning Human Understanding*. Hume presents a battery of arguments against the claim that the testimony of others provides anything like enough evidence to justify belief in supernatural miracles.

To begin with, Hume reminds us of our enthusiasm for the bizarre and our eagerness to believe that a miracle has occurred. Often, we don't even bother to look for an alternative explanation.

In his book, *The Missionary Position*, Christopher Hitchens provides a nice illustration of how our eagerness to believe can cause us to overlook more mundane explanations. Hitchens relates that while making a documentary about Mother Teresa, Malcolm Muggeridge became convinced that he had witnessed a miracle. The story of Teresa's miracle spread rapidly and the media quickly snapped it up. But what really happened? Ken Macmillan, one of those involved in making the documentary, explained:

During *Something Beautiful for God*, there was an episode where we were taken to a building that Mother Teresa called the House of the Dying. Peter Chafer, the director, said, 'Ah, well, it's very dark in here. Do you think we can get something?' And we had just taken delivery at the BBC of some new film made by Kodak, which we hadn't had time to test before we left, so I said to Peter, 'Well, we may as well have a go.' So we shot it. And when we got back several weeks later, a

month or two later, we are sitting in the Rushes
Theatre at Ealing Studios and eventually up came the
shots of the House of the Dying. And it was surprising.
You could see every detail. And I said, 'That's amazing.
That's extraordinary.' And I was going to go on to say,
three cheers for Kodak. I didn't get a chance to say that
though, because Malcolm, sitting in the front row, spun
round and said: 'It's divine light. It's Mother Teresa.
You'll find that it's divine light, old boy.' And three or
four days later I was being phoned by journalists who
were saying things like: 'We hear you've just come back
from India with Malcolm Muggeridge and you were
the witness of a miracle.'[6]

In his rush to embrace the miraculous, Muggeridge
entirely overlooked the correct explanation for what had
occurred: the film crew had merely been experimenting
with a more sensitive type of film.

Hume also points out that people often have an interest
in propagating stories of miracles and the supernatural,
whether or not the stories are true. Television programmes
that explore the 'bizarre and unexplained', full of hype and
sensationalism, tend to get much higher ratings than those
that take a more sceptical view. They therefore generate
more advertising revenue for the television company, so
there is a strong financial incentive for television compa-
nies to make programmes that are heavily biased towards
the miraculous.

Hume also reminds us how easy it is to forge miracles.
Of course modern-day illusionists like David Blaine and
David Copperfield are easily able to convince people that
they have witnessed something miraculous. Blaine can

levitate himself an inch or two off the pavement while his audience walks around him; Copperfield flies over audiences, and can even fly inside a sealed container preventing the use of hidden wires. Many of these faked miracles are, frankly, at least as convincing as most that are supposedly genuine. A bleeding statue can quickly be mocked up with a bottle of chilli sauce. Ghostly knockings in séances are easily contrived (one well-known medium even learnt to crack her toes under the table in response to her gullible punters' questions: one crack for yes, two for no). As there is fame and money to be had from faking miracles, we can confidently expect many people to try. And, given our credulity and the ease with which miracles can be faked, we can also expect a great many people to be taken in. Their tales will be retold over and over by people who have an interest in enhancing them, focusing on those details that seem most extraordinary and leaving out anything that might cause others to be more sceptical.

So, concludes Hume, we should expect to hear a great deal of testimony about miracles anyway, whether or not they really happen. The fact that there is a great deal of testimony does not, by itself, provide us with much in the way of evidence that miracles occur.

Hume also draws our attention to the fact that we have, in any case, considerable evidence that the universe is governed by strict laws that do not allow miracles to happen. So when, for example, someone tells us that they have witnessed their dead auntie suddenly materialising in their living room, we must weigh up the evidence on either side. What is more likely, asks Hume: that the laws of nature really have been overturned and Auntie has been resurrected, or that this witness has either been deceived in some way (perhaps they were hallucinating, for example), or else is deliberately deceiving us? In every case, insists Hume, the latter conclusion invariably turns out to be the more reasonable. It is always more probable that a miracle hasn't occurred than that it has.

> When anyone tells me that he saw a dead man restored to life, I immediately consider it in myself, whether it be more probable, that this person should either deceive or be deceived, or that fact, which he relates, should have happened. I weigh one miracle against the other; and according to the superiority, which I discover, I pronounce my decision, and always reject the greater miracle. If the falsehood of his testimony would be more miraculous than the event which he relates; then, and not till then, can he pretend to command my belief or opinion.[7]

## *Hume on miracles 'cancelling out'*

Hume has another argument up his sleeve. He reminds us that each religion has its own store of miracles upon which it can draw. Muslims, for example, believe that Mohammed flew from Mecca to Jerusalem during the night. Hindus believe that Krishna, the second person in the Hindu trinity, was resurrected after death. Yet all these religions contradict each other. For example, Christians believe that Jesus was the son of God whilst Muslims and Hindus deny this. Given their fundamentally conflicting claims, only one (if any) of these religions can be true. But then the support that each set of miracles provides for its own particular religion is cancelled out by the numerous miracles supporting the others.

> [L]et us consider, that, in matters of religion, whatever is different is contrary; and that it is impossible the religions of ancient Rome, of Turkey, of Siam, and of China should, all of them, be established on any solid foundation. Every miracle, therefore, pretended to have been wrought in any of these religions (and all of them abound in miracles), as its direct scope is to establish the particular system to which it is attributed; so has it the same force, though more indirectly, to overthrow every other system. In destroying a rival system, it likewise destroys the credit of those miracles, on which that system was established.[8]

The situation, Hume suggests, is similar to a jury being presented with conflicting witness testimony: if one witness swears that Bob committed a robbery with him on Monday night, but the other maintains that Bob was at home with him watching TV, then we are not yet in a position to place much trust in either witness.

Perhaps Hume slightly overstates his case here. The early Christians accepted miracles associated with other faiths, but put them down to the activity of demons, not God. For such Christians, the existence of these other non-Christian miracles was entirely consistent with their own faith. So, the credibility of Christian miracles need not be undermined by miracles belonging to other faiths.

However, what does appear to be true is that if there are equally plausible-looking miracles associated with each of the different faiths, then they don't give us any reason to suppose that any particular religion is true – their effect is cancelled out. On this point, surely, Hume is correct.

## Other evidence

Hume may reject testimony of the miraculous, but let's not forget that there are other forms of evidence. What if you were to witness a miracle with your very own eyes? There might also be hard, physical evidence of a miracle: for example, an X-ray showing that a tumour has miraculously vanished. This sort of evidence could conceivably justify belief that a miracle has taken place.

Suppose, for example, that angel-like beings started appearing all over the Earth, often in front of large crowds of people. They float in the air, tell us that they are messengers from God, and perform seemingly miraculous deeds, such as raising the dead. If all this happened, would it still be irrational to believe that supernatural miracles occur?

Of course, no matter how much evidence might accumulate, it would still be possible for sceptics to insist that we were being fooled. 'Perhaps,' they might say 'these "angels" are really aliens who, with their advanced technology, are able to perform miracle cures. So nothing they do actually violates any law of nature. There's nothing supernatural about these beings. As Arthur C. Clark points out, any sufficiently advanced technology is indistinguishable from magic.'

But while it is always possible, with a little ingenuity, to come up with some sort of naturalistic explanation for unusual events, such explanations might become increasingly strained as more and more evidence stacked up in support of the supernatural. The most plausible thing to believe might eventually be that the laws of nature really were being violated and supernatural miracles were taking place.

## Did the Christmas miracle happen?

Whilst we can conceive of a situation in which it would be rational to suppose that supernatural miracles were taking place, is there, in actual fact, anything like enough evidence to warrant belief in supernatural miracles? In particular, is there sufficient evidence to justify the belief that the Christmas miracle occurred and Jesus really was born of a virgin?

I suggested earlier that perhaps a cumulative case might be made for that conclusion. There is a great deal of testimony in the Bible about Jesus's miraculous nature and Christians continue to report miracles and cures being done in his name. Against this, we must balance Hume's points about human gullibility, our fondness for miracles and the ease with which they can be faked. We should remember that X-rays can be muddled, for example, and that people suffering from cancer can go into spontaneous remission without divine help.

There are, in addition, two further reasons why we ought, perhaps, to be at least cautious about accepting at face value the Biblical account of Jesus's birth.

First, there is absolutely no mention of either the immaculate conception or the virgin birth in the earliest

Gospel, Mark. The Christmas miracle only makes an appearance in the later Gospels (and even John omits the virgin birth). Was Mark simply ignorant about these extraordinary events? Or did he not think them worth mentioning?

Second, at the time the Gospels were written, there was a widespread and well-established pagan tradition of retrospectively attributing divine conceptions and virgin births to mythic heroes and famous figures. Even Plato's biographer, Diogenes Laertius, suggested that Plato was both divinely conceived and born of a virgin.[9]

Knowing all this, how reasonable is it to believe that Jesus really was born of a virgin? You should draw your own conclusion.

## *The importance of the Christmas miracle*

How important is it to the Christian faith that the supernatural miracles reported in the Bible really happened?

For some, the claim that Jesus performed genuinely supernatural feats is absolutely central to their belief. If there was no virgin birth and Jesus was not God incarnate then, they would say, Christianity is a false religion, period. We might still view Jesus as an important teacher in the way Muslims do, for example. But to be a Christian, surely, one must believe that Jesus was rather more than a great teacher – after all, even an atheist can accept that.

On the other hand, perhaps the importance of the Biblical miracles can be overstated. Some Christians view supernatural miracles as largely an irrelevance: what does it matter if Jesus really did raise the dead and cause the blind to see? Emphasising the hocus–pocus in the story of Jesus's life is, they would suggest, likely to make us overlook what is truly important: the message.

Certainly, many Christians would want to remind us of the miraculous in the everyday. They would urge us not to forget that creation, life, human existence and birth are also important miracles in their own right. As C. S. Lewis puts it, religious miracles 'are a retelling in small letters of the very same story which is written across the whole world in letters too large for some of us to see.'[10]

---

1 Thomas Paine, *The Age of Reason*, Part I, quoted in Alexander Waugh, *God* (London: Headline, 2002), p. 197.

2 Woody Allen, 'The Scrolls' in *Complete Prose* (London: Picador, 1997), p. 37.

3 *See* 'God is my Dentist' in *Whoa!*, 24 September 1999 or at www.getting it.com/article/94.

4 R. F. Holland, 'The Miraculous', in *Against Empiricism* (Oxford: Basil Blackwell, 1980).

5 Doron Nof and Nathan Paldor, 'Are There Oceanographic Explanations for the Israelites' Crossing of the Red Sea?', quoted in Theodore Shick, Jr, and Lewis Vaughn, *How to Think About Weird Things*, 2nd edn (Mountain View, California:
Mayfield Publishing, 1995), p. 21.

6 Ken Macmillan, quoted in Christopher Hitchens, *The Missionary Position* (London, Verso, 1995), pp. 25–6.

7 David Hume, *An Enquiry Concerning Human Understanding* (1777), in *Enquiries Concerning Human Understanding and Concerning Principles of Morals*, ed. L. A. Selby-Brigge, 3rd edn, revised by P. Nidditch (Oxford: Oxford University Press, 1975), section X, Part I, p. 116.

8 Ibid., p. 121.

9 See Randel Helms, *Gospel Fictions* (New York: Prometheus, 1998), p. 50.

10 C. S. Lewis, 'Miracles' in *God in the Dock* (Glasgow: Collins & Sons, 1979), p. 16.

# The Santa Claus Puzzle

*Here's a famous, mind-boggling, logical puzzle that occasionally crops up on undergraduate finals papers.*

## Santa's beard

'Santa Claus has a white beard.' Is this true, false or neither?

University of London, BA Philosophy examination (2001), Logic and Metaphysics, Question 3.

Existence is one of those properties that cause philosophers a great many headaches. Particularly bothersome are things that *don't* exist, such as Santa Claus.

Think about the sentence: 'Santa Claus has a white beard.' Is this sentence true, false, or neither?

Intuitively, it's true: Santa does have a white beard, doesn't he? But therein lies the puzzle. For it seems the one thing this sentence cannot be is true.

Why so? Well, 'Santa Claus' is a proper name. And the job of a proper name within a sentence is, presumably, to refer to something or someone. For example, if I say, 'Jack is tall,' I use the name 'Jack' to refer to someone. What I say is true if the person I refer to is tall, and false otherwise. But what if there is no such person as 'Jack'? What if I'm using the name idly, without referring to anyone in particular? Then, surely, what I say is neither true nor false. The sentence might just as well contain a gap where the name is, like this: '— is tall,' and this doesn't say anything at all. But then the same, it seems, must be true of the sentence, 'Santa Claus has a white beard.' It must, in effect, say the same as '— has a white beard,' which says nothing at all.

## Why it isn't true that Santa doesn't exist

The mystery doesn't end there, for the same problem crops up with respect to the sentence: 'Santa Claus does not exist.'

Again, this sentence is true. But how come? If the job of the proper name 'Santa Claus' within a sentence is to refer, and there's nothing for it to refer to, then it cannot do its job. So 'Santa Claus does not exist' should no more succeed in saying something true than '— does not exist'.

In fact, in this case the puzzle is even more acute, for while we might, in desperation, be tempted to admit that 'Santa Claus has a white beard' is neither true nor false, we can't plausibly say that about 'Santa Claus does not exist'. Very clearly, this sentence *is* true.

For some of us, such puzzles are endlessly fascinating. Others find them about as entertaining as repeatedly slamming your head in a door. For the amusement of the former group only I briefly present two attempted solutions.

## *A solution*

You might suggest that in fact the name 'Santa Claus' does refer to something. Not Santa Claus, obviously, for he doesn't exist. Rather, the name refers to our idea of Santa Claus: that's to say, our idea of a red-suited, white-bearded fat man who rides a flying sleigh.

This suggestion gets round the problem of the missing reference – the reference is now the idea, which does exist, but it fails to explain how 'Santa Claus does not exist' can be true. For, of course, if when we say 'Santa Claus does not exist', we are saying that our idea of Santa Claus does not exist, then what we say is not true, but false. As I say, our idea of him *does* exist.

## *A more sophisticated solution*

The sentence 'Santa Claus has a white beard' is true. That's because when we talk about Santa, we engage in a pretence. We have created a fictional character. And, within the pretend world within which this fictional being exists, he does in fact have a white beard. So what we say is 'true' in the sense that it's true within the pretence.

This would explain, incidentally, why the sentence 'Santa Claus is over six feet tall' is, unlike a sentence concerning a real individual, neither true nor false. Because we have never specified how tall Santa is to be within this pretend, fictional world, there simply is no fact of the matter as to how tall he is.

We may have explained how 'Santa Claus has a white

beard' can be true. But what about: 'Santa Claus does not exist'? How can this sentence be true?

Well, perhaps, in this case, we are making a pretend reference and then going on to say that that pretend reference really does not exist. So again, what we say is true. Problem solved!

Or is it?

# ❦ 10 ❦

## Christmas and Tradition

*Christmas is one of the few traditions that most Westerners still share. Could the loss of such traditions and the values they help to inculcate be responsible for the West's alleged moral decline?*

Christmas is a time at which many of us come together, in churches to join in the carol singing, as families to exchange gifts and share a meal, in schools to watch our children perform in nativity plays, and at parties. Christmas is a tradition that reminds us that we are not isolated individuals, hermetically sealed off from each other, but members of a wider community. It can, if only for a short time, give us a sense of 'belonging'.

Not so very long ago, whole communities were immersed in such traditions. People came together, not just annually, but once a week. Religious festivals provided the framework for the year, marked our birth and death, and gave meaning to our lives. It was also to our religious traditions that we looked for moral guidance. In fact, there was hardly an aspect of life that was not touched by the traditions that bound us together.

Many lament their passing. Here, for example, is the chief rabbi Jonathan Sacks.

A vision once guided us, one that we loosely call the

Judaeo-Christian tradition . . . It did not answer all questions . . . But it gave us moral habits. It gave us a framework of virtue. It embodied ideals. It emphasized the value of institutions – the family, the school, the community – as vehicles through which one generation hands on its ideals to the next. In its broad outlines it was shared by rich and poor alike . . . You could catch traces of it from pub to pulpit to cricket matches. It bound us together as a nation and gave an entire society its bearings. That tradition has been comprehensively displaced.[1]

Sacks argues that it is this loss of tradition, and particularly the moral authority and values embedded within the Judaeo-Christian tradition, that is largely responsible for the moral malaise which, Sacks suggests, is now consuming the West. As the tradition has withered, so the bonds that once held us together as communities have fallen away. We have become free-floating, isolated individuals set adrift within a moral vacuum. No one is morally answerable to anyone but him- or herself. As a result, the social fabric is unravelling, and immorality and crime are spiralling out of control.

In his Richard Dimbleby Lecture in 2003, Rowan Williams, the new archbishop of Canterbury, expressed similar concerns. 'Let me put it provocatively,' he said. 'We are no longer confident of educating children in a tradition.' And yet such traditions, he argued, are necessary if we are not to end up thinking of everything solely in terms of our own individual desires. Without a religious tradition, society degenerates into nothing more than a market place governing the competing short-term interests and preferences of individuals. Larger questions simply disappear from view.

> The great revolt against traditional authority in the seventeenth and eighteenth centuries was a necessary moment, because tradition was understood as the way in which the past dominated the present . . . But what about the person who is now able to inhabit a tradition with confidence, fully aware that it isn't the only possible perspective on persons and things, but equally aware that they are part of a network of relations and conventions far wider than what is instantly visible or even instantly profitable, and this network is inseparable from who they concretely are? I suspect that many of us would recognise in this more of freedom than of slavery, because it makes possible a real questioning of the immediate agenda of a society, the choices that are defined and managed for you by the market.[2]

Indeed, Williams believes that it is only from the perspective of a religious tradition that questions about the meaning of our lives are even raised, let alone answered.

## The Enlightenment rejection of tradition

What is the root cause of the collapse of religious tradition? Sacks argues that a critical wrong turn was taken during the seventeenth and eighteenth centuries, during the Enlightenment, when philosophers started to place far more importance on the individual, and his or her powers of reason. For example, Kant, one of the greatest of the Enlightenment philosophers, believed that, through the application of pure, unadulterated reason a person could work out what is right and what is wrong without having to appeal to any external religious authority at all.

Sacks believes that Kant's influence has been malign, and points out that, once morality has become the individual's call, then it is but a short step to it becoming purely a matter of individual and arbitrary whim. 'I ought' becomes 'I want'.

The columnist and social commentator Melanie Phillips concurs. As direct consequence of Enlightenment thinking, she says, '[w]ithin three centuries . . . morality became a matter of individual will, preference, emotion or decision . . . The concepts of right and wrong became meaningless because they no longer applied to objective principles. There were no moral standards any more, only choices.'[3]

Sacks, Williams and Phillips all draw heavily on the work of the philosopher Alisdair MacIntyre. MacIntyre argues that while Enlightenment philosophers might have thought they were discovering, through their own individual application of reason, timeless truths, they were doing no such thing. Morality cannot be conjured out of thin air by an individual insulated from tradition. Indeed, there is no escape from tradition: 'What I am . . . is in key part what I inherit, a specific past that is present to some degree in my present. I find myself part of a history and that is generally to say, whether I like it or not, whether I recognize it or not, one of the bearers of a tradition.'[4] In fact, argues MacIntyre, whatever forms of reasoning we employ are themselves born of and dependent upon tradition. So it is actually *impossible* to do what philosophers such as Kant attempted to do, which is to apply reason on a purely individual basis: 'All reasoning takes place within the context of some traditional mode of thought.'[5]

## *Losing the plot*

MacIntyre also emphasises the way in which morality is intertwined with and dependent upon stories:

> I can only answer the question 'What am I to do?' if I can answer the prior question, 'Of what story or stories do I find myself a part?' We enter human society, that is, with one or more imputed characters – roles which we have been drafted – and we have to learn what they are in order to be able to understand how others respond to us and how our responses are to be construed. It is through hearing stories . . . that children learn or mislearn both what a child and what a parent is, what the cast of characters may be in the drama into which they have been born and what the ways of the world are. Deprive children of stories and you leave them unscripted, anxious stutterers in their actions as in their words.[6]

Rowan Williams echoes MacIntyre's remarks about the importance of a shared narrative: 'People learn how to tell the story of their own lives in a coherent way when they have some broader picture to which to relate it. You can only tell the story of your own life, it seems, when it isn't just your story, or even the story of those immediately close to you.'[7]

In the absence of any traditional, shared story to sustain them, morality and meaning wither away. According to many, the story that is retold and celebrated at Christmas, of Christ's birth and life, and of course the wider story of God's plan for the world, is the story within which Christian morality is rooted. As people increasingly lose touch with that story, they are, quite literally, losing the plot.

## *The rise of relativism*

Sacks and Phillips both believe that the collapse of religious tradition has been accompanied by – and indeed exacerbated by – the growing, malign influence of trendy relativist thinking, particularly in schools and universities.

Relativism is the view that what's true for one person or culture may be false for another. There's no absolute moral truth, just differing opinions, all of which are equally valid.

Take, for example, the practice of female circumcision. Many Westerners are horrified by it. The practice does, after all, result in a loss of sexual pleasure for the woman concerned, it can be extremely painful, is often performed by individuals with no medical training, leading to urinary and gynaecological problems, and is forced on young children without their consent. It should, many argue, be stopped. But of course those who practise female circumcision (many of whom come from the Sudanese culture) think it's entirely morally permissible. So who is right?

According to the relativist, *both* points of view are correct. Relative to many Westerners, it is 'true' that female circumcision is wrong; but relative to the Sudanese, who practise it, it is equally 'true' that it's morally correct. All moral positions are true, for the people who hold them.

At this point you might be tempted to ask: but what is the *real* truth? Setting aside the fact that people can hold, and justify, differing points of view, which point of view is actually, objectively correct?

According to the relativist, there is no such thing as objective, non-relative moral truth. That's precisely their point. Truth is relative.

If that sounds odd, then consider an analogy. Native Australians are fond of witchetty grubs, large fat larvae that are eaten live and raw. Most non-aboriginals, on the other hand, find eating the grubs an absolutely revolting experience. So who is correct? Are witchetty grubs *really* revolting, or aren't they? The answer, it seems, is that there is no answer to this question. The deliciousness or otherwise of the grubs is not an objective, intrinsic property of them, like their size or their weight, but is relative to whoever is eating them. Now according to the moral relativist, much the same is true of moral properties. Moral properties are not objectively, independently 'there anyway', but, like the revoltingness of witchetty grubs, they are rooted in our subjective reaction to what we experience.

Melanie Phillips believes that the decline of traditional,

religious values in education has in part been brought about by the rise of relativism, which, particularly since the 1960s, has been pushed by woolly-minded teachers in the classroom. As a consequence, she says, 'Everyone has become their own individual arbiter of conduct with no-one else permitted to pass judgement.'[8] Under the guise of 'tolerance', 'open-mindedness' and 'freedom', teachers have been spreading highly destructive relativist attitudes in the classroom. If little Johnny thinks that stealing from other children is morally acceptable, then, for him, it is. Who are we to judge?

Of course, the relativist is correct that we should in many cases respect those whose opinions on moral issues differ from our own. We should also acknowledge that we're fallible and that our views may not always be right. We should not just assume that we have nothing to learn from others.

However, to respect the beliefs of others and admit our own fallibility is one thing; to accept that there is no objective, external truth of the matter is, as Phillips correctly points out, quite another. We can embrace tolerance, open-mindedness and freedom without embracing relativism.

Nevertheless, relativism has, according to many thinkers, now become *the* dominant 'politically correct' philosophy right across the West. The American academic Allan Bloom writes that '[t]here is one thing a professor can be absolutely certain of: almost every student entering university believes, or says he believes, that truth is relative.'[9] Marianne Talbot, a lecturer in philosophy at Oxford, reports that her students 'have been taught to think their opinion is no better than anyone else's, that there is no truth, only truth-for-me. I come across this relativist view constantly – in exams, in discussion and in tutorials – and I find it frightening: to question it amounts, in the eyes of the young, to the belief that it is permissible to impose your views on others.'[10]

Phillips suggests that we are now seeing the results of this philosophy in the spiralling levels of crime and a shallow 'me-first' culture that trumpets the rights of the individual while ignoring or even denying the existence of any responsibility to others. If all moral opinions are valid, then who is to judge if I think it is morally acceptable to vandalise a phone box or steal a car?

## *Rehabilitating tradition*

The vision I have been sketching – of a culture within which our children are set adrift, with no story by which to make sense of their lives, and with no external tradition to provide them with a moral compass – is not entirely one of despair. Sacks, in particular, is clear that we can rebuild. Like Williams, Sacks thinks we need to re-root our children in religious tradition. Across the West, this idea is attracting and uniting a great many diverse thinkers and is even beginning to shape government policy. In the UK, for example, the Labour Government's enthusiasm for 'faith' schools is undoubtedly partly motivated by a sense that religious traditions and the communities they bind together are an important corrective to the increasingly fragmented Western culture of the individual.

If we are to rebuild, then traditions that are still widely observed, such as Christmas, could provide an ideal foundation. We might perhaps start by reminding children of the religious story behind this yearly event, and of its moral and spiritual significance. The same might be said of the festivals belonging to other religious traditions.

## *Tradition and authoritarianism?*

But isn't there a problem with this call for a return to religious tradition and authority? It would be easy to caricature the kind of pro-tradition philosophy shared by MacIntyre, Williams, Phillips and Sacks as a rather crude form of authoritarianism in disguise. For aren't they recommending, in effect, that we should all stop thinking for ourselves and start deferring to whatever tradition dictates? Aren't they suggesting that we all become moral sheep, blindly treading whatever path tradition lays down? What about individual autonomy? What about freedom of thought?

In fact, all of the above writers are very clear that they are *not* recommending that we become mere slaves of tradition. They acknowledge that the mere fact that an attitude is traditional certainly doesn't guarantee that it is correct. What they reject is the view that each individual can and should attempt to build their own moral system from scratch, from within. Traditions can and should sometimes be criticised and changed. But it is only *from the standpoint of a shared tradition* that the resources required for proper criticism are even available.

## *Deference to tradition versus freedom of thought*

While no one is recommending blind, unwavering loyalty to whatever tradition dictates, nevertheless Sacks and Phillips are clear that they believe that on moral questions children should, in the first instance, adopt an attitude of deference to what Phillips calls 'external authority'. Proper criticism of tradition and authority, and independence of thought, are only to be allowed – indeed are only possible – among those who have already been properly immersed within the tradition.

Of course, most of us would agree that very young children cannot enter into a particularly meaningful debate about whether or not, say, stealing from other children is wrong. They just have to be told. And we can also agree that no one, of any age, should simply be free to do whatever they want.

But what about older children and their freedom of thought? At what point is that to be encouraged? When would Sacks and Phillips allow us to ask why we should believe this rather than that? At what point are we to be allowed to start thinking for ourselves?

In fact, none of the writers we have looked at is particularly clear about this. Sacks says:

> We need to set foot within a practice, finding our way round it from the inside. This presupposes distinctive attitudes: authority, obedience, discipline, persistence and self-control . . . There is a stage at which we put these rules to the test. We assert our independence, we challenge, ask for explanations, occasionally rebel and

try other ways of doing things. Eventually we reach an equilibrium . . . For the most part . . . we stay within the world as we have inherited it . . . capable now of self-critical reflection on its strengths and weaknesses, perhaps working to change it from within, but recognizing that its rules are not a constraint but the very possibility of shared experiences and relationship and communication . . . [A]utonomy takes place *within* a tradition.[11]

While Sacks clearly acknowledges the importance, in a mature and fully socialised individual, of a critical and reflective stance towards his or her own tradition, he stresses that the individual must first have been fully steeped in that tradition, and emphasises the importance of authority and obedience in the earlier stages of assimilation. At quite what point Sacks is willing to allow us to express some independence of thought is unclear. At five? At ten? At fifteen? Not until we go to university? Sacks doesn't say.

## Glover on the perils of authoritarianism

Whatever Sacks' view, is it entirely sensible to encourage, not just very young children, but also older children and even young adults, to adopt an attitude of deference to authority and tradition when deciding what they should think on moral issues? Probably not very sensible, is my guess.

One of the great lessons of the twentieth century is that society has an in-built problem with moral sheep –

tend naturally to defer to authority on moral matters. This was demonstrated particularly vividly by the psychologist Stanley Milgram back in the 1950s. Milgram set up an experiment to establish what strength of electric shock an ordinary American citizen would administer to a stranger if asked to do so by a white-coated authority figure. Astonishingly, the majority of subjects tested, while in most cases clearly extremely distressed by what they were doing, were willing to go to 400 volts, beyond the point at which they believed the person to whom they were administering shocks had been killed. Despite feeling that what they were doing was wrong, they found the pressure to defer to the authority figure overwhelming. What Milgram revealed was that the soldiers who ran Auschwitz and said they were 'only obeying orders' weren't inhuman monsters; they were just like the rest of us.

Milgram showed that human beings tend to lack the inner resources to identify and stand up for what is right when pitted against a malign authority. Given this potentially catastrophic tendency, should we really be *encouraging* children and young adults to adopt such unquestioning attitudes to authority? Rather, shouldn't we be encouraging them, from as young an age as possible, to take on the responsibility for making their own moral decisions, making sure they have the critical and emotional resources to discharge that responsibility properly?

As the philosopher Jonathan Glover explained in an interview in the *Guardian*:

> If you look at the people who sheltered Jews under the Nazis, you find a number of things about them. One is that they tended to have a different kind of upbringing

from the average person, they tended to be brought up in a non-authoritarian way, brought up to have sympathy with other people and to discuss things rather than just do what they were told.[12]

Glover adds, 'I think that teaching people to think rationally and critically actually can make a difference to people's susceptibility to false ideologies.'

No doubt Sacks would agree with Glover that people should be taught to think for themselves, though within the tradition and not from the outset. As I have pointed out, the question is: when exactly do we start teaching them to think for themselves? Glover's research into the horrors committed during the twentieth century seems to suggest that if we do not start encouraging independence of thought until early adulthood, we may have left it far too late.

## Muddling relativism and liberalism

Graham Haydon, a lecturer in philosophy of education, also warns of the perils of getting children to adopt an attitude of deference to authority and tradition:

It still must be said forcefully that accepting uncritically what someone tells you because they are seen to be in authority is not a good thing . . . Doing what is right cannot be a matter of doing what one is told. Schools must produce people who are able to think for themselves what is right . . . It will not take an exceptionally clever pupil, or an exceptionally bolshie one, to ask: 'How do we know this is right or that is wrong?' Any pupil who is being taught to think ought to be asking such questions. And the same pupil ought to see that 'Because I say so' is not an acceptable answer. Nor is 'because these are the values of your society'. When exposed to a little more teaching of history, perhaps, this pupil will see that by such an argument the value of slave states and Nazi states would have to be endorsed.[13]

Haydon's comments mesh with Glover's concerns about the risks attached to an authoritarian moral upbringing. Yet this liberal attitude outrages Melanie Phillips, who condemns his reasoning as 'specious and dangerous'. Why? Because, according to Phillips, Haydon is promoting relativism. He is suggesting that we should teach children that there is no fact about what is right and what is wrong.

But of course, Haydon is suggesting no such thing. The liberal position (that we ought, as far as possible, to encourage individuals to think for themselves on moral questions), should not be muddled with the relativist position (that all moral points of view are equally 'true'). There is nothing inconsistent about, on the one hand, rejecting relativism and taking the view that what is right and wrong is absolute – a matter of objective fact – while, on the other hand, encouraging individuals to work out what those objective moral facts are.

The problem is that, in her haste to decry liberal attitudes to moral education, Phillips entirely misses this point. She supposes that 'relativism . . . flows inevitably from the destruction of all external authority and the relocation of that authority within the child'. That is simply not true.

## Conclusion

At Christmastime, many people are put back in touch, if only fleetingly, with a great religious tradition that once bound together an entire community.

Some see the decline of religious tradition as a good thing. Such traditions, they suggest, were all about enforcing conformity. The ties that bound us together were oppressive. It is better, they say, that we are now free to think for ourselves and to express differing points of view.

On the other hand, religious traditions can bring a sense of belonging and community. And, many argue, they provide us with the kind of grand narrative without which we are morally at sea.

There may be some truth in both these points of view. My argument has been that, even if there are aspects of religious tradition that we should aim to rehabilitate, this still leaves open important questions about the extent to which individuals, and especially children, should be encouraged to think freely and for themselves, particularly on moral issues.

---

1 Jonathan Sacks, *The Politics of Hope* (London: Jonathan Cape, 1997), pp. 260–1.

2 Rowan Williams, Dimbleby Lecture 2003.

3 Melanie Phillips, *All Must Have Prizes* (London: Warner Books, 1998), p. 197.

4 Alisdair MacIntyre, *After Virtue* (Notre Dame, Indiana: University of Notre Dame Press, 1981), p. 206.

5 Ibid.

6 Ibid., p. 210.

7 Williams, op. cit.

8 Phillips, op. cit., p. 116.

9 Allan Bloom, *The Closing of the American Mind* (New York: Simon and Schuster, 1987), p. 25.

10 Marianne Talbot, quoted in Phillips, op. cit., p. 221.

11 Sacks, op. cit., pp. 176–7.

12 Jonathan Glover, 'Into the Garden of Good and Evil', *Guardian*, 13 October 1999.

13 Graham Haydon, quoted in Phillips, op. cit., p. 221–2.

# 11

## The Christmas Turkey

*A famous illustration popular with philosophy lecturers.*

Ted the turkey arrives at the turkey farm and discovers on his first morning that he is fed at 8 a.m. Being a cautious turkey, Ted doesn't jump to any conclusions. He makes a series of observations, recording what happens each morning, on wet days and on fine, on Mondays and Tuesdays, and so on. Ted finds that, whatever the circumstances, he is always fed at 8 a.m. And so, finally, Ted satisfies himself that he has collected enough data to infer 'I am always fed at 8 a.m.' Unfortunately, it is now Christmas Eve and Ted is not fed but has his neck wrung.

This cautionary tale – a favourite of philosophy students – is often attributed to the philosopher Bertrand Russell. In fact, Russell's original example concerned a chicken and made no mention of Christmas Eve.[1] But the moral remains the same: it doesn't matter how much evidence we might accumulate about what has happened in the past, it can't provide us with any logical guarantee about the future.

Of course, when it comes to arriving at beliefs about the

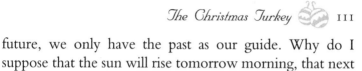

future, we only have the past as our guide. Why do I suppose that the sun will rise tomorrow morning, that next time I turn on a tap water will come out, and that the next duck I see will quack? Because that's what has always happened up to now.

But there's no logical contradiction involved in supposing that, although water has come out whenever the tap has been turned on in the past, the same may not happen tomorrow. Perhaps the world will suddenly go crazy. Maybe sand will suddenly start pouring from taps, ducks will miaow and the sun will be replaced by a giant, million-mile-wide inflatable panda. There's no *guarantee* such things won't happen.

Of course, scientists also rely on the same potentially error-introducing form of reasoning. They must base their theories about how the universe functions on what they have observed up to now. Yet their theories concern the laws of nature: laws that should hold for all times and places, including the future. So their scientific theories about the laws of nature are inevitably somewhat speculative. Our scientists could be wrong.

People often make a dire mistake when they first come across this point about the fallibility of scientific reasoning. They conclude that, as scientific reasoning is not 100 per cent reliable, therefore it must be 100 per cent unreliable. They suppose that there's really no reason at all to believe that ducks will continue to quack, and that the sun will rise tomorrow morning. Our beliefs about what will happen in the future – including our scientific beliefs – are nothing but guesswork!

Those who would like to see science taken down a peg or two often find this line of thought appealing. But it involves a muddle. The tale of the Christmas turkey nicely illustrates the point that scientific reasoning can and does go astray. But that doesn't mean it isn't fairly reliable. True, there's no *logical guarantee* that the future will resemble the past, but, as Russell also reminds us, we may still have good grounds for supposing it will.[2]

---

1 Bertrand Russell, *The Problems of Philosophy* (Oxford: Oxford University Press, 1998), p. 53.
2 On the other hand David Hume has an argument that appears to show that we really do have no reason at all to suppose the sun will rise tomorrow. Hume may indeed be correct. My point is that the story of the Christmas turkey doesn't justify us in drawing this radical conclusion. See Chapter 14 of my book, *The Philosophy Gym* (London: Headline, 2003) for an explanation of Hume's argument.

# 12

## Faith in the Twenty-first Century

*We are encouraged to see Christmas as a time to reaffirm our Christian faith, if we have one. But what is faith, exactly? And is it necessarily a good thing? In the current climate, post 11 September, is it wise to encourage people to throw reason to the wind and* just *believe?*

Children hear the word 'faith' used frequently around the Christmas period: in school assemblies, at the carol service, on Christmas cards and in the nativity play. It's a word that, for many of us, comes with a built-in breakfast-cereal glow, like 'trust', 'honesty' and 'peace'. Such words tend to evoke a warm, comfortable vision of people living contentedly together.

Many, on the other hand, are deeply suspicious of the term. For 'faith', they read 'wishful thinking', or perhaps even worse: 'mind-control'. Many see faith as something deeply dangerous: a tool by which people can be manipulated into committing all sorts of horrendous acts.

Which of these contrasting perspectives on faith is more accurate? Is faith a force for good, or a force for evil?

## *Varieties of faith*

Of course, the term itself has several different meanings. First, there are religious faiths, plural. A faith, in this sense, is a religious system of thought, like the Christian faith, the Jewish faith, and the Muslim faith.

Second, faith is a kind of belief held in the absence of good supporting arguments and/or evidence. This is the sort of faith that people invoke when they assert that belief in God is a matter of faith, not reason.

Third, we talk about having or placing our faith in someone or something. This is faith as a form of trust. You can have faith in your friends: that they will be supportive of you when you need their help. You may have faith in your car: that it will get you to your destination. You might also place your faith in God.

These are clearly three different sorts of 'faith'. They may coincide, but not necessarily. Someone might, for example, have the first and third forms of 'faith', but not the second. They may believe in the Christian God, but also think they possess very good grounds – perhaps even irrefutable proof – that this God exists. If so, then they need not bother with 'faith' in the second sense. But they may still have 'faith' in the third sense: they may place their trust in God, much as a child might place its trust in its parents.

So when we ask, 'Is faith a good thing?' we are really asking at least three different questions:

Are religious faiths a good thing?

Is faith (as opposed to reason) a good thing?

Is placing one's trust in God a good thing?

Let's take a brief look at each of these questions in turn.

## *1. Religious faiths*

Are religious faiths a good thing? Not even the most cynically minded atheist can seriously deny that religious faiths can be and sometimes are a force for good. Around the globe, people of different faiths can be found helping others, sometimes at great cost and even risk to themselves. They provide relief at home and abroad, helping in times of drought, famine and war, providing education, clean water and other much-needed resources to people who would otherwise not receive this help. It is precisely *because* they have embraced a faith that many of these people do what they do.

There is also a growing body of evidence that embracing a religious faith can be good for you. Numerous studies indicate that those who believe tend to lead healthier, longer and more contented lives than those who don't. Mormons, in particular, seem to enjoy very good health: their rates of cancer and heart disease are less than one half those found in the wider population.[1]

One possible explanation for this is that a religious faith can provide both psychological comfort and a network of physical, emotional and even spiritual support. The bereaved may find solace in the belief that there's an afterlife. Ex-drug addicts testify how their religious faith strengthened their resolve to overcome their dependency. And because faith-based communities tend to be highly supportive of their members, it would be surprising if that did not have some positive impact on their health and happiness.

So yes, religious faiths can be a force for good. But it would be absurd to pretend that they have not also, as a matter of historical fact, been a force for evil. Faiths can be divisive. Many of the great conflicts around the world, from Northern Ireland to the Middle East, are actually defined in terms of faith. Religious faiths have also inspired a great deal of intimidation and violence and, in some cases, have a poor track record on tolerance.

## 2. *Faith and reason*

The second sort of faith is often contrasted with reason

When you believe something with reason, you possess good grounds for supposing your belief to be true.

Take, for example, my belief that there is a tree outside my office. I can't now see the tree, but it's reasonable for me to suppose it's still there. I saw it only a minute ago. And there's no reason at all to suppose that someone has somehow managed to remove it while I have been sitting here. So I'm justified in believing the tree is still there.

Surely, I'm also justified in believing that Japan exists, despite the fact that I have never been there myself. I have seen innumerable TV programmes about Japan. I have met people who claim to be from Japan and who all speak with a characteristic accent. And I have seen countless maps on which Japan clearly appears. Some of my relatives even claim to have been there. So, again, I have excellent reason to suppose Japan exists.

I'm also justified in believing that the battle of Hastings

took place in 1066. I have read about the battle in a number of books written by reputable authors, so I have pretty good reason to suppose it's true. Maybe this belief of mine isn't quite as well confirmed as my belief that Japan exists. After all, historians can and do make mistakes. But it is, nevertheless, a fairly reasonable thing for me to believe.

Of course, while I'm justified in holding these beliefs – while I have good reason to hold them – it's possible I'm mistaken. Most if not all of our beliefs about the world are open to at least some doubt. Even my belief that Japan exists. It's just possible that there has been some huge and elaborate conspiracy to dupe me into thinking Japan exists when in fact it doesn't. Perhaps my whole life has been controlled by forces intent on deceiving me, as in the film *The Truman Show* (in which Truman, the central character, discovers that his entire life has been contrived as part of a TV soap opera). The point is that, although it *could* turn out to be true that Japan doesn't exist, it's very unlikely. The reasonable thing for me to believe is that it does. For I have powerful evidence that it does, and hardly any evidence to suggest that it doesn't.

### REASONABLENESS COMES IN DEGREES

Notice that reasonableness comes in degrees. Beliefs can be more, or less, reasonable. My belief that Japan exists is very reasonable indeed. So too are my beliefs that the Earth revolves around the sun, that Elvis Presley is dead, and that there are no fairies at the bottom of my garden. Other beliefs lie in the middle range: there is some reason to suppose they are true, but perhaps not enough to warrant belief. For example, there is some reason to believe that there is life on other planets. We know there are millions of other solar systems, many of which would probably be capable of producing and sustaining life. It's not wholly unreasonable to suppose that life has evolved elsewhere. But perhaps that doesn't amount to sufficient evidence to justify belief in extraterrestrial life.

Towards the bottom of the scale there are beliefs for which not only is there very little supporting evidence but considerable evidence to the contrary. The beliefs that Elvis is alive and well, that fairies exist and that the world is run by a secret cabal of Martian imposters all fall into this category (despite what you might read on some internet sites).

So there is a scale of reasonableness: beliefs can be more or less reasonable, depending on the evidence.

## *Scale of Reasonableness*

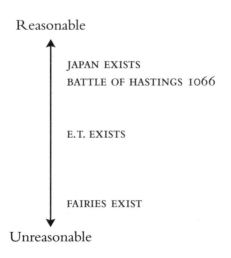

Reasonable

JAPAN EXISTS
BATTLE OF HASTINGS 1066

E.T. EXISTS

FAIRIES EXIST

Unreasonable

To qualify as reasonable, a belief must at least fall within the top half of the scale.

Now where on this scale does belief in God lie? Does it feature down at the 'fairies exist' end of the spectrum? Does it lie somewhere in the middle, along with the extraterrestrials? Or is towards the top of the scale, perhaps as high as my belief that the battle of Hastings took place in 1066, or even as high as my belief that Japan exists?

In my experience, most people who believe in God consider their belief to be quite reasonable, that's to say, at least as reasonable as belief in extraterrestrial life, and perhaps even as reasonable as my belief that the battle of Hastings took place in 1066. Certainly, that's what most of the Christians I have asked have said. Not one has ever supposed that belief in God is no more reasonable than, say, belief in fairies. They're always confident that belief in God is *fairly* high up the scale.

## A FURTHER DISTINCTION

If most Christians claim that belief in God is quite reasonable, then what do they mean when they say that it is a matter of faith, not reason?

That's not entirely clear. Some appear to mean that while there are fairly good grounds for believing in God, it is a 'faith position' in the sense that it is 'not proved' – by which they mean that these grounds for belief fall short of being *absolutely* conclusive and irrefutable.

This is a not uncommon way of using the term 'faith', but it is *not* the kind of faith that is usually contrasted with reason. In fact, even scientific theories are 'faith positions' according to this use of 'faith'. The theory that the Earth goes round the sun rather than vice versa qualifies as such because there is still, after all, the tiniest possibility of our being mistaken. A belief can be very reasonable indeed while still being 'not proved'.

The kind of faith that is contrasted with reason is different. It is the sort of faith that Luther seems to have had in mind when he said, 'Faith must trample underfoot all reason, sense, and wish to know nothing but the word of God.'[2] One just believes, completely irrespective of whatever reason or the evidence might suggest. This sort of faith could be termed blind faith.

Unfortunately, these two forms of 'faith' – the it's-fairly-reasonable-but-I-could-conceivably-be-mistaken sort of faith and blind faith – are often confused. In fact, those who believe in God sometimes slide between these two senses of the term without realising they have done so.

### THE DANGERS OF BLIND FAITH

It is of course the extreme, blind form of religious faith – the kind that is entirely disengaged from reason – that those who warn of the perils of faith are most concerned about. It's the blind form that Richard Dawkins is speaking of when he says: '[It] is capable of driving people to such dangerous folly that [it] seems to me to qualify as a kind of mental illness.'[3] It is the blind form that the philosopher Daniel Dennett warns us about when he comments: 'there are no forces on this planet more dangerous to us all than the fanaticisms of fundamentalism.'[4] It is the blind form that Bertrand Russell has in mind when he says:

If you think your belief is based upon reason, you will support it by argument rather than by persecution, and will abandon it if the argument goes against you. But if your belief is based upon faith, you will realize that argument is useless, and will therefore resort to force either in the form of persecution or by stunting or distorting the minds of the young in what is called 'education'.[5]

We are all acutely aware of how hazardous blind religious faith can be. Once people of an extreme faith have got it into their heads that they should do some terrible deed, there's little we can do to persuade them out of it. They, quite literally, won't listen to reason.

## 3. *Faith as a form of trust*

The third form of faith mentioned right at the beginning of this chapter is faith as a form of trust. Is this form of 'faith' in God a good thing?

We constantly place our faith and trust in those around us. I have faith in the postman: that he will deliver my letters and not chuck them in the bin. I have faith in my bank manager: that she will deal with me honestly and won't disappear with all my money. Indeed, without this sort of trust in others, life would become impossible.

So it appears that placing our faith in others is generally a positive, life-enhancing and even admirable thing to do. But then, isn't it, by the same token, positive to place our faith in God? That is what many would argue.

### THE SANTA CASE

This particular justification for religious faith is confused. First of all, the 'trust' form of faith is concerned with the character of a person, not their existence. When I place my trust in my bank manager, my faith doesn't concern her existence. That she exists is perfectly obvious: she's standing right there before me. Rather, my faith is in her *character*. I trust that she really is as honest and straightforward as she appears to be.

Imagine the following case.

Dad is short of money and Christmas is coming. His two children are eagerly awaiting their presents, but he cannot afford to buy them any. Still, he's not disheartened. In fact, he remains upbeat. Dad knows there is little reason to suppose that Santa Claus exists, but nevertheless places his faith in Santa Claus to produce presents for the children on Christmas Day.

'Don't worry, children,' says Dad. 'I know that Santa is a good person. I feel quite sure that he *will* bring you lots of presents.'

Dad is placing his faith, his trust, in Santa's good character to deliver on Christmas Day. But is this father's 'faith', a 'faith' that he also encourages in his children, really a positive and admirable thing?

I think not. The problem is that, *unless Dad has fairly good grounds for supposing Santa exists*, his faith in Santa's good character is downright stupid, and, in this case, potentially upsetting for other people.

In short, to place your faith in the goodness of a person is generally only positive and admirable if you have fairly good reason to suppose the person in question actually exists. If there isn't good reason to suppose God exists then it certainly doesn't follow that placing your faith in his goodness must be a positive, life-enhancing thing to do.

Perhaps it can be a good thing to place one's trust in God. The fact is that this particular argument, as it stands, doesn't establish that point.

## Let's be clear

Many would argue that Christmas is a time at which children should be immersed in 'faith'. But if that is so, then we ought to be clear about the sort of 'faith' we are encouraging them to embrace. Theists certainly should not use 'blind faith' as a way of dodging awkward atheistic arguments and then, when the atheist has left the room, revert to saying that belief in God is 'quite reasonable just not proven'. Many different things go by the name of 'faith'. Not all of them are intrinsically bad. Some forms of faith are, perhaps, to be encouraged. Certainly, some are fairly innocuous. But there are also varieties of faith that are downright dangerous. If we are going to expose children to 'faith', we clearly have a duty to be honest and open about the kind of 'faith' we have in mind.

1 See Roger Highfield, *Can Reindeer Fly?*, (London: Phoenix, 2001), Chapter 10.
2 Alexander Waugh, *God* (London: Headline, 2002), p. 267.
3 Richard Dawkins, *The Selfish Gene*, 2nd edn (Oxford: Oxford University Press, 1989), p. 330.
4 Daniel Dennett, *Darwin's Dangerous Idea* (Harmondsworth: Penguin, 1995), p. 516.
5 Bertrand Russell, *The Quotable Bertrand Russell*, ed. Lee Eisler (Buffalo, NY: Prometheus, 1993) p. 261.

# 13

## Carving the Roast Beast

*Every year in the UK, more than 25 million turkeys are killed for our Christmas dinner. Is this mass slaughter justifiable merely to satisfy our preference for a certain kind of meat? Shouldn't we be carving nut cutlets instead?*

The Wilson family are sat around the Christmas dinner table. Dad is carving the turkey when he glances a little apprehensively at his eldest daughter, Gemma.

MR WILSON: Some turkey, Gemma?

GEMMA: Of course not. You know I'm a vegetarian.

MRS WILSON: Only since last week. And it's Christmas. Can't you join in just this once?

GEMMA: No. It's morally wrong to eat meat. I'm not going to do something morally wrong just to make you happy.

Much the same conversation will be familiar to parents around the world. Teenagers are increasingly becoming vegetarians, often on moral grounds. It can be irksome for the parents: special meals have to be cooked and time and effort put into making sure that their offspring get a balanced diet.

Still, while Gemma's views might be inconvenient, that doesn't make them mistaken. And in fact Gemma does have some rather good arguments up her sleeve.

Gemma points to the carcass that Mr Wilson is patiently deconstructing with his electric carving knife.

GEMMA: Are you aware just how miserable a life that poor creature led? It was raised in a shed, along with thousands of other birds. It never saw the light of day. It never even saw a tree or a blade of grass. How can you justify such cruelty? Just so that you can enjoy the short-lived pleasure of shoving its cooked muscles into your face?

MR WILSON: Well, there's no need for that sort of talk, is there? You're putting us off our dinner.

GEMMA: You *should* be put off your dinner!

MRS WILSON: I'm afraid, Gemma, you're mistaken. This turkey had rather a lovely life, in fact. Aunt Freda raised it on her farm by hand and slaughtered it herself. She assures me it never suffered at all, in life or in death. I went to all the trouble of getting it for you so you wouldn't have to worry about animal cruelty. So why don't you have some?

Mrs Wilson might seem to have dealt with Gemma's objections, but Gemma is insistent that, no matter what sort of life the turkey had, it is *still* wrong to kill and eat it.

GEMMA: Look, I don't care whether it had a lovely life or not. That's really not the issue. The issue is that it was a living thing capable of enjoying life. That life was cut short just so that you could enjoy the taste of its flesh with your sprouts. That's morally wrong!

MR WILSON: But *why* is it wrong? After all, it's not like killing a human being, is it?

GEMMA: Isn't it?

MR WILSON: Obviously not! Human life is sacred. But animals are different, aren't they? It's OK to kill and eat *them*.

GEMMA: Well, yes, I know that's your *opinion*. But look, not so very long ago, people thought it was OK to discriminate against other races, didn't they? White people enslaved black people, and treated them as their personal possessions. They thought it was 'just obvious' that it's morally permissible to discriminate between whites and blacks. But they were mistaken about that, weren't they?

MR WILSON: Of course. That was just prejudice.

GEMMA: And you also think it's wrong for men to discriminate against women, don't you?

MR WILSON: Absolutely. I disapprove of both racism and sexism. I'm not prejudiced.

GEMMA: Yet you are guilty of *speciesism*, and that's just another example of prejudice. You just don't recognise that you are prejudiced. You may not be prejudiced against those of a different race or a different sex. But you are prejudiced against those of a different species. You think human beings are more deserving of our concern and respect than pigs and cows and chickens, simply because they are human. That's just like a white person saying that whites are more deserving of concern and respect simply because they're white. It's nothing more than a prejudice!

Mrs Wilson is incensed at the suggestion that she is prejudiced and bangs down her serving spoon in protest.

MRS WILSON: We're *not* prejudiced, Gemma! After all, there are good reasons for discriminating between humans and other species. Of course it was wrong for men to discriminate against women and whites to discriminate against blacks. The differences between black people and white and men and women do not justify any difference in treatment. What is relevant about sex or skin colour when it comes to the issue of whether or not people should be allowed to hold certain jobs or to vote? Nothing at all. But some differences *do* justify discrimination.

GEMMA: Such as?

MRS WILSON: Well, take children and adults, for example. Adults don't let children vote or drive or hold down positions of responsibility. And why not? Because the differences between adults and children justify our discriminating in that way. Children aren't clever or mature enough to do those things.

GEMMA: I see. So what's the difference between humans and other species that justifies us treating them so differently? Why is it morally wrong to kill and eat a human being . . .

MR WILSON: Oh Gemma, do you *have* to bring up these revolting analogies at the dinner table?

GEMMA: . . . but not morally wrong to kill and eat this turkey?

MR WILSON: Because *it's a turkey*!

GEMMA: But that's no answer, is it? You're like a slave owner who, when asked why it is acceptable to enslave black people, replies, 'Because *they're black*!'

It appears that Gemma is correct: the mere fact that the turkey belongs to another species does not, by itself, appear to justify the difference in treatment. Merely to appeal to a difference in species would seem, on the face of it, to be just another form of unreasoned bigotry against those that are different. It would, indeed, appear to be a form of prejudice akin to racism.

But then what does justify the very different way in which we treat other species? That's not such an easy question to answer.

Mr Wilson puts down his electric carving knife and stares for a moment or two at the dismembered corpse on the plate before him. Then he tries the following suggestion.

> MR WILSON: Very well, the reason that it is morally acceptable to kill and eat this turkey, but not a human being, is that turkeys are, frankly, pretty dim. A human being is a highly intelligent creature. Humans have language, don't they? They have a highly sophisticated range of emotions. A turkey is, by comparison, mentally unsophisticated. I have never heard of a talking turkey or a turkey enjoying a night out at the opera, have you? *That's* the relevant difference between humans and turkeys. That's why we can eat them.

This is a highly popular justification for the kind of discrimination we practise against other species. I suspect most people, if asked to justify eating meat, would probably very quickly come up with a justification along similar lines.

## *The mentally impaired*

But unfortunately, as Gemma now explains, her father's justification runs up against a very well-known counter-example.

> GEMMA: Look, suppose some babies are born that are severely brain-damaged. Their fathers were all accidentally irradiated in a nuclear accident. That damaged the genetic code handed down to their children. As a result, these children are not very bright. They will never learn to speak. In fact, they are never going to be any more mentally sophisticated than, say, your average turkey. Now, how do you think we should *treat* these babies?
>
> MR WILSON: Well, we should look after them, of course, and make sure they get the best quality of life possible.
>
> GEMMA: *But why not kill* and eat them?!
>
> MRS WILSON: Kill and eat babies?
>
> MR WILSON: Oh, honestly . . .
>
> GEMMA: But look, you said the reason it's OK to kill and eat this turkey, but not a human, is that the human is much smarter. Well, these babies may be human, but they are no smarter than turkeys. So, *by your own reasoning*, it should be morally acceptable to kill and eat them!
>
> MR WILSON: But babies are *human*, for God's sake!

Human life is sacred.

GEMMA: But that's just *speciesism*! *Why* is human life sacred and animal life not?

The philosopher Peter Singer agrees with Gemma about that charge of speciesism. Singer asks us to imagine a case in which a child is born with massive, irreparable brain damage. The damage is so severe that the child can never be more than a 'human vegetable', and will certainly never reach the level of mental sophistication achieved by the kind of animals we habitually kill and eat. The parents, realising there is no hope of improvement, and being unwilling to spend, or to ask the state to spend, the large amounts of money needed annually for proper care of the infant, request that the doctors kill their child painlessly. Singer asks:

Should the doctor do what the parents ask? Legally the doctors should not, and in this respect the law reflects the sanctity of life view. The life of every human being is sacred. Yet people who would say this about the infant do not object to the killing of nonhuman animals. How can they justify their different judgements? . . . The only thing that distinguishes the infant from the animal, in the eyes of those who claim it has a 'right to life,' is that it is biologically a member of the species Homo Sapiens. But to use *this* difference as the basis for granting a right to life to the infant and not to the other animals is, of course, pure speciesism. It is exactly the kind of arbitrary difference that the most crude and overt kind of racist uses in attempting to justify racial discrimination.[1]

## *Social bonds*

There is a lull in the conversation as the Christmas crackers are pulled and party hats donned. The pause gives Mr Wilson time to think up a different justification.

MR WILSON: Very well, I admit that it's not just the fact that we are smarter than other species that matters. For, of course, we're not only brighter, we also enter complex social relationships with each other, relationships that no animal can enter into.

GEMMA: What sort of relationships?

MR WILSON: Well, there are *social bonds* that tie us humans together, aren't there? After all, we as a family are very strongly tied to each other. We have obligations to each other that we do not have to other human beings.

GEMMA: What sort of obligations?

MR WILSON: Well, as your father, I have an obligation to care for you. That is an obligation I do not have to other children. I have stronger obligations to my immediate family than I do to more distant relatives. And I have stronger obligations to my immediate community than I have to complete strangers.

GEMMA: I see. So it's OK to eat complete strangers with whom we're not bonded, then?

MR WILSON: No, no, of course not! I still have a duty to strangers precisely because they are still members of human society, with all the moral and political obligations that brings.

MRS WILSON: I think your father is right. What we owe to others depends not just on what they are, but on how we are socially bound together.

Gemma's younger sister Ellen, who has been following the conversation with interest, chips in.

ELLEN: Yes, that's true, isn't it? And we have a much stronger obligation to our dog Blackie because he's socially bonded to us, though not in the way a human being is, of course. That's why it would be wrong of us to kill and eat him. But killing and eating a turkey? That's fine!

The suggestion that we have weaker moral obligations to other species because there are not the same social bonds between us has been carefully developed by the philosopher Mary Midgley.[2] The suggestion certainly does have some intuitive appeal. Surely we do have stronger obligations to those with whom we share the deepest bonds, such as our immediate family.

Still, the suggestion runs into difficulties, as Gemma now points out.

GEMMA: You say that the reason it's OK to kill and eat a turkey but not a human is because of the social bonds between us. But then a severely mentally impaired human is no more able to enter into those relationships than a turkey. So why isn't it OK to kill and eat the mentally impaired human?

MR WILSON: It's true: we cannot enter into the same social relationships with the mentally impaired that we can with other human beings. But still, there are *emotional* ties that bind us to them, aren't there? *That's* why we have a much greater moral obligation to humans than turkeys, irrespective of how smart they are.

GEMMA: But that can't be the reason why it's OK to kill and eat the turkey, because racists could use that argument too!

MR WILSON: Why?

GEMMA: Well, if white people don't feel the same emotional bonds and ties to black people as they do to each other – and of course sometimes they don't – and if white society was arranged so that the whites had very few social bonds with black people, then, according to you, their racism would be perfectly acceptable!

Again, it seems to me that Gemma is right. If our social and emotional ties with other humans are what give us moral obligations to them, then what about deeply racist societies where these bonds don't exist? What about a society in which one race feels no more socially or emotionally bonded to another than we do to animals? (Arguably, such societies have actually existed.) Mr Wilson would have to say that, in such a society, it's morally acceptable for one race to kill and eat the other. But that's absurd.

## *Potential*

What then *does* justify the way in which we discriminate between mentally impaired humans on the one hand and animals on the other? The philosopher Roger Scruton suggests that the relevant difference is not a difference in what these beings *are*, but in what they have, or had, the *potential* to be.

> It is in the nature of human beings that, in normal conditions, they become members of a moral community, governed by duty and protected by rights. Abnormality in this respect does not cancel membership. It merely compels us to adjust our response . . . It is not just that dogs and bears do not belong to the moral community. They have no potential for membership. They are not the *kind of thing* that can settle disputes, that can exert sovereignty over its life, that can respond to the call of duty or take responsibility on a matter of trust.[3]

It is the fact that human beings are *normally* able to enter into social and moral relations that's important. If, because of an impairment, some aren't able to enter into such relations, that does not matter. They still qualify for a much higher level of moral respect and concern than that given to other animals.

Has Scruton succeeded in explaining why we are not guilty of speciesism in discriminating as we do?

I do not believe so. Consider a hypothetical case. We are presented with two groups of what appear to be mentally impaired humans. They are severely impaired. They will never learn to speak. They are never going to be any more emotionally or intellectually sophisticated than the average pig. Examine these two groups and you will find them indistinguishable: both are intellectually undeveloped and for the same immediate reason – their genetic code is slightly different from ours. It is this genetic difference that accounts for their intellectual deficit.

Now, suppose that one group have this genetic code because their fathers were accidentally irradiated in a nuclear accident. So these individuals would have been intelligent if their fathers had not been irradiated. The potential was there. But because of the accident they were born abnormal.

The second group is genetically – and, indeed, physically – indistinguishable from the first. However, the second group is non-human. In fact, they are extraterrestrials. They are the offspring of a parallel species from another planet. Because of their different environment, this parallel species has failed to evolve as we have. These individuals are, in fact, *normal* for their species. The *potential* to be smart was never there.

Now ask yourself the following question. Morally speaking, would we be justified in discriminating between these two groups of molecularly indistinguishable individuals? In particular, would it be acceptable for us to kill and eat the second group, but not the first?

Surely not! Morally, what's important about these individuals is what they *are*, not what they might have been. Suppose that, because of a muddle, the two groups are mixed together. Would we be justified in researching their ancestry to find out which are abnormal humans and which are normal extraterrestrials, so that we might care for the former and send the latter to the abattoir? Of course not. That would be a gross form of speciesism.

But notice that if Scruton were correct, then we *would* be justified in killing and eating the second group but not the first. For the second group are 'normal' for their species and never had the potential to be the same as us. So Scruton's justification of why it is OK to kill and eat other species produces a highly counter-intuitive result.

A defender of Scruton might, I suppose, suggest that the second group *does* have the potential to evolve. For if the mentally challenged extraterrestrials were to go through several million years of the right sort of evolution, they might end up as intelligent as we are. So we shouldn't eat them. The problem with this move is that the same is probably true of pigs. Given the right sort of environment and several million years, pigs might well evolve to be as smart as us. The potential is there. So, if *that's* what Scruton means by 'potential', it probably is morally wrong to eat pigs. Yet that is exactly what Scruton denies.

## *Appeals to the Bible*

The rest of the Wilson family are becoming frustrated with Gemma. They feel quite sure that it is morally acceptable to kill and eat a turkey, but they are also finding it difficult to explain why.

Then Grandma Wilson makes a suggestion.

GRANDMA: Look, Gemma, *of course* it's permissible for us to kill and eat turkeys, pigs, bulls, chickens and any other creature we fancy, for that matter. After all, it says so in the Bible, doesn't it? God gave us permission. God said to Noah, 'Every moving thing that liveth shall be meat for you.'

GEMMA: But I don't believe in God.

GRANDMA: You don't?

GEMMA: No. And in any case, I am not sure how even a Christian can be quite so confident about the Bible. After all, in Leviticus, it says that it is acceptable to own slaves, so long as they come from neighbouring countries.

GRANDMA: It does?

GEMMA: Yes, it does. And of course the slave owners seized on that passage. 'Look, it says it's OK in the Bible!' they said. Now you don't, I take it, think it morally acceptable to own slaves?

GRANDMA: Er . . . no. I don't.

GEMMA: Yet you are happy to use the same sort of Biblical justification for eating meat!

Yet again, Gemma appears to be right: even if the Bible is a reliable source of moral knowledge (and of course we would need good reason to suppose that it is if we are to have good reason to trust what it says), the fact is that even Christians ignore what the Bible has to say about keeping slaves. But then how can they consistently appeal to the Bible in order to defend the killing and eating of animals?

## *Health and design*

Mrs Wilson suggests that Gemma should eat some turkey because it's good for her.

>    MRS WILSON: Please eat some turkey. It's full of protein. You *need* meat to stay healthy.
>    GEMMA: No I don't. There are millions of people across the world living healthy lives without meat. Countless Buddhists, Jains and Hindus do without eating animal flesh. And they are perfectly healthy.

Again this is perfectly true. We don't need to eat meat. But still, as Mr Wilson reminds Gemma, eating meat is a natural part of our diet.

>    MR WILSON: But we're *designed* to eat meat, aren't we? We have canine teeth, for goodness sake: teeth designed to rip animal flesh. It's *natural* for us to eat meat!

Again, this is a popular justification for meat eating. But, of course, the fact that something comes 'naturally' to us is hardly a moral justification for doing it.

>    GEMMA: All sorts of things seem to come naturally to humans, from starting wars to persecuting those that are different from us. You would not, I take it, attempt to justify jealousy and hatred on the grounds that these emotions are natural?
>    MR WILSON: Well, no. I guess not.

GEMMA: Then why do you appeal to the naturalness of eating meat in order to justify it? I don't see what 'naturalness' has got to do with it.

Mr Wilson is also beginning to wonder what naturalness could have to do with it. Mrs Wilson passes round the roast potatoes.

MRS WILSON: But most of the animals that we eat would not have existed at all if they hadn't been raised for the dining table. This turkey, for example, had an enjoyable life that it would not have had if Aunt Freda hadn't bred it to be eaten.

GEMMA: But that would justify eating the mentally impaired if they were bred for the dining table, wouldn't it? Suppose we started breeding mentally impaired humans to be eaten. These humans wouldn't have had a life at all if they weren't going to be eaten. But clearly that wouldn't justify our killing and eating them. The fact that they were bred for that purpose is beside the point.

## *They eat us; why shouldn't we eat them?*

However, Ellen thinks there's some justice in our killing and eating other animals. For after all, they kill and eat each other and, on occasion, us too.

ELLEN: But, Gemma, animals kill and eat animals, don't they? So why shouldn't we kill and eat them?

GEMMA: The fact that they kill and eat each other is

irrelevant. First of all, animals have to eat each other to survive, don't they? A tiger can't survive on grass, can it? Second, animals have no sense of right or wrong so they cannot be blamed for what they do. They are like children. Sometimes young children do things they shouldn't. They lash out at each other without thinking, for example. Now you wouldn't justify lashing out at *them* on the grounds that *they* do it, would you?

ELLEN: Well, no, I wouldn't.

GEMMA: So why is it any more acceptable to suggest that the reason it is OK to kill and eat other animals is that they kill and eat animals?

ELLEN: Hmmm. I'm not sure . . .

The Wilson family fall silent. They stare at the turkey getting cold on the plate before them.

MRS WILSON: I have some nut cutlets in the fridge.

---

1 Peter Singer, *Animal Liberation*, 2nd edn (London: Pimlico, 1995), p. 18.

2 *See* Mary Midgley, *Animals and Why They Matter* (Athens, GA: University of Georgia Press, 1983).

3 Roger Scruton, *Animal Rights and Wrongs*, 3rd edn (London: Metro, 2000), pp. 54–5.

# 14

## The Carol Service

*Each Christmas, churches that usually stand empty are suddenly brimming with people happily singing carols, kneeling for the prayers and celebrating along with the priest or vicar. Many of them are atheists. Isn't there something deeply hypocritical about non-Christians celebrating Christmas in this way? Or is Christmas something we should all be able to participate in, whatever our beliefs?*

Some Christians are annoyed by the presence of atheists at Christmas services. 'If they don't believe in God,' they ask, 'then why do they come at all? They're hypocrites, standing awkwardly at the back and hoping we won't notice them. This is one of the most important events in the Christian calendar and it's being treated as a concert – they're only here for the music and the lights.' On the other hand, many Christians don't just tolerate non-Christians at these events; they positively encourage them to come along.

So is Christmas just for the Christians?

## *Pascal on going through the motions*

The philosopher Blaise Pascal[1] thought that while there might not be convincing evidence of God's existence, nevertheless it is sensible to make oneself believe in God. Pascal suggests that we approach belief in God as a wager, and that we calculate how to bet by looking at what we stand to win or lose.

First, suppose we believe that God exists. And suppose we are wrong: there is no God. Then we have lost very little (not much more than a lie-in on Sunday morning). If there is a God, on the other hand, then the pay-off is huge: we receive eternal life.

Now suppose we bet the other way: we believe there is no God. If we are correct, then we gain little (little more than that Sunday morning lie-in). On the other hand, if we don't believe and there *is* a God, then our loss is huge: we face eternal damnation.

So, argues Pascal, belief in God is the best bet. Belief in God costs us little, and if we win, we win big. Fail to believe, and we risk losing a great deal.

But what if we find ourselves unable to believe? What if, try as we might, belief eludes us? What are we to do then?

Pascal suggests the solution is to *act* as if one believes. Play out the rituals of belief: attend church, kneel and say the prayers. Go through the motions. Eventually, Pascal suggests, belief will follow.

Of course, approaching religious belief as a wager is a rather cynical attitude to take. But still, many Christians might agree with Pascal that, if they can at least persuade atheists to attend church services and go through the motions of belief, there is a good chance that many will end up acquiring the beliefs themselves. If we want to convert atheists, Christians may reason, then we should encourage them to join in at Christmas time.

## *Frazer and Wittgenstein on the role of ritual*

Still, for someone who doesn't yet believe in God, mustn't religious ritual and prayer seem rather pointless? Why sing God's praises if we think he doesn't exist? Why bother praying if we suppose no one is listening?

The philosopher Wittgenstein presents some interesting arguments about the value that such rituals can have, irrespective of actual belief. I have in mind his examination of the mythologist Sir James Frazer's investigation into magical thinking, *The Golden Bough*. Frazer argues that the magical thinking of 'primitive' people really constitutes a naive theory about how the universe operates. Take, for example, a tribesman who ritualistically pushes a knife into an effigy of his enemy. Does this tribesman actually believe that his knife will have an effect on his adversary? Does he believe that by stabbing the doll he may cause his enemy to die? Frazer answers 'yes'. The tribesman performs this ritual because he believes in what Frazer calls the law of similarity: he believes that like produces like, and that effects resemble their causes. Of course, scientific sophisticates like ourselves know better. But many 'primitive' cultures go through a stage in which they believe in the law. They try to achieve an end by imitating what they desire. This, according to Frazer, explains why people sprinkle water on the ground to make the rain fall, push knives into effigies of their enemies, and enact successful hunting scenes before they embark on a real hunt.

It appears that the ancient Scandinavian custom of burning Yule logs (which has since become incorporated into our own Christmas traditions) also fits Frazer's account of magical thinking. In the depths of winter, the Scandinavian pagans feared the sun would not return in the spring, and apparently believed that by ritually burning a log (which, like the sun, burns warm and bright) they could magically make the summer sun return.

Wittgenstein rejects Frazer's explanation of all this doll-stabbing and water-sprinkling. According to Wittgenstein, the tribesman who pushes a knife into an effigy of his enemy doesn't *really* believe that he may thereby cause his enemy's death. After all, says Wittgenstein, '[t]he same savage who, apparently in order to kill an enemy, sticks a knife through a picture of him, really does build his hut of wood and cuts his arrow with skill and not in effigy.'[2] This is a telling criticism. If the tribesman *truly* believed in the law of similarity, as Frazer suggests, then he would also build his hut in effigy, expecting a full-size hut magically to appear. But he has no such expectation. In fact, this sort of ritualistic behaviour is not really 'primitive' at all. It is not something we have left behind. Wittgenstein points out that, no matter how scientifically sophisticated we are, we still engage in it: we kiss images of the ones we love and tear up photos of those we hate. But why? 'Burning in effigy. Kissing the picture of a loved one. This is obviously not based on a belief that it will have a definite effect on the object which the picture represents. It aims at some satisfaction and it achieves it. Or rather, it does not aim at anything; we act in this way and then feel satisfied.'[3]

The reason we kiss images, tear up photographs, throw darts at images of political leaders and so on, is not that we suppose our actions will have a real effect on the people these images represent (if they did, then Margaret Thatcher, a favourite dartboard pin-up of the 1980s, should now be peppered with tiny holes). We do what we do because of the emotional value it has for us. Such actions can console us. They can make us more resolute. They can inspire us.

Wittgenstein would no doubt say the same about the burning of Yule logs. It is not that the Scandinavians actually believed that, by burning a log, they could cause the sun to return. They burnt the log because of the effect it had on them. It touched something deep within them; they would burn the log and then, as Wittgenstein puts it, 'feel satisfied'. That is why the practice continues even today.

## *The magical and spiritual*

So such symbolic and ritualistic actions can have great emotional value, whether or not we believe in their practical efficacy or the literal truth of the doctrines associated with them. They are, arguably, an important part of being human, giving us the opportunity to express deeply felt emotions that would otherwise remain stifled. It is not a stretch, I think, to say that they put us in touch with our spiritual side.

In the West, the great established religions once provided the framework within which such ritualistic activity took place. As the practice of religion has declined, that opportunity has been lost. The magical and spiritual side of our emotional nature has been suppressed and forgotten. Many would say that is a good thing – it shows that we are 'progressing', that we are becoming more scientific and rational. But is this necessarily progress? If Wittgenstein is correct, ritualistic behaviour is part of our nature and therefore not something we can leave behind. Try to suppress it and, I suspect, it will simply re-emerge in a different form. One of the reasons why New Age religions and cults are booming is that they offer to reconnect us with this side of our emotional character.

But then, if Wittgenstein is correct, perhaps even an atheist might gain some spiritual value from going through the religious rituals associated with Christmas? For example, they might derive real comfort from kneeling with the rest of the congregation and praying for peace, even if they think there is no God to answer their prayers. They may still leave the service feeling moved and uplifted. The spiritual side of their nature may still be engaged.

## A sense of community

There is another reason why non-believers might gain from Christmas traditions: they offer one of the few opportunities we have left to come together as a community. They give us a sense of solidarity with our fellow man, a sense of belonging, as the philosopher Peter Singer points out: 'Although I am firmly non-religious, and lack even a Christian family background, when I stand with the other parents at the Carol Night held by my children's school . . . the effect of everyone singing together can lead to a strong emotional response that makes me feel the importance of being part of that community.'[4] I suspect that it is not a fondness for candles and carol music, but this 'strong emotional response', combined with the emotional value of ritual, that explains why many non-Christians find themselves drawn to church at Christmas time.

As we saw in Chapter 10, many would argue that it is the loss of such traditions, and the sense of community and belonging they help engender, that are responsible for the 'moral malaise' that is, it's alleged, consuming society. If this is true, then perhaps we should encourage people to involve themselves in these traditional, communal events, whether or not they happen to be specifically Christian. By involving themselves in the rituals and traditions of Christmas, individuals may still, like Peter Singer, get a real sense of belonging.

The 'strong emotional response' of which Singer speaks, combined with the emotional power of magical ritual and symbolism, combine to form a highly intoxicating brew. Almost all of us have felt its power at some time or other. I remember that, as a small boy, I was emotionally almost overwhelmed by a baptismal service; being surrounded by my entire family, the collective singing, the rituals and the setting all combined to produce an experience as intense as any I have ever felt.

Let's not forget, of course, that these emotional tools can also be used for evil: to inspire not love, but fear and hatred, especially towards those who do not fall within the charmed circle of our community. In the wrong hands – in the hands of a malevolent religious leader, for example – these tools become terrible and fearsome weapons. If we are going to encourage their use, we must make *very* sure they're handled responsibly.

## Christmas and the pagans

Sometimes, midway through a carol service or midnight mass, congregations are reminded from the pulpit not to forget the *real* meaning of Christmas. At this point there is usually some awkward staring at hands and shuffling of feet, for it is generally assumed that the 'real' meaning of Christmas must be a specifically Christian meaning, a meaning presumably lost on the unbelievers at the back.

We can all agree, of course, that the 'real' meaning of Christmas does not reside in the commercial racket that has largely taken over our festivities. But is the 'real' meaning of Christmas specifically Christian?

It's occasionally suggested that it is actually the Christians who are the interlopers at a midwinter festival with its roots in the great pre-Christian pagan religious cults. In Christ's time, the birth of many more or less interchangeable pagan god-men was widely celebrated on 25 December, including Dionysus (in Greece), Osiris (in Egypt), Mithras (in Persia) and Bacchus (in Italy). The significance of 25 December is that for a long time it marked the winter solstice: the shortest day, the point at which the sun is born again for another year (our calendar has since changed and the solstice now falls on 21 December). Incidentally, all the pre-Christian god-men listed above were also miraculously born of virgin mothers. So was Buddha, who also pre-dates Christ and, it was believed, was divinely conceived in the womb of the virgin Maya. Buddha's birthday? Again, 25 December. The Scandinavians also celebrated 25 December as the birthday of Freyr, the son of their supreme god, Odin.

Now there is nothing in the Bible to suggest that Jesus was born on 25 December, or even in winter for that matter. The decision to mark his birth on that date was made several hundred years after his death and was probably influenced by its solar and pagan religious significance. 'So the Christians,' some non-Christians complain, 'like the Grinch, *stole* Christmas. They stole it from the pagans. If Christmas has a real meaning, it's essentially pagan.'

But whilst Christmas undoubtedly does owe something to pre-Christian pagan traditions, and some of its trappings may be borrowed from them (as I mentioned earlier, Yule logs are pagan), that doesn't make Christmas itself pagan. After all, almost every tradition borrows from earlier traditions in various ways. Christmas is not unique in that respect. Yale University's traditions owe something to Oxford's. That doesn't make Yale Oxford.

## Christmas for everyone?

If the real meaning of Christmas is neither Christian nor pagan, then what is it?

There is no consensus about that, even among Christians. For some, it involves believing in the literal truth of the nativity story: Jesus really was divinely conceived and born of a virgin. There really was a star, three kings, gifts of gold, frankincense and myrrh.

However, many Christians no longer take this story literally, at least not in all its details. Some have even been known to question the virgin birth. But if these details are removed, what is left?

A great deal, of course. The residual meaning upon which almost all of us can agree is that Christmas is a celebration of peace and love, and a time to think of others, especially those less fortunate than ourselves. It is a time when we come together, when we feel solidarity and empathy with the rest of humanity. Much of the true meaning of Christmas is open to everyone, whatever their religious beliefs.

Traditionalists may be horrified at the suggestion that we, in effect, make Christianity an optional Christmas extra. Isn't this an example of pick'n'mix religion? We take the bits we like (the 'Christmas spirit', the coming together of the community) and discard the rest. But Christmas always was a pick'n'mix event. Its traditions, beliefs and customs are in many cases borrowed.

Christmas has an appeal that reaches far beyond the Christian. In an age when religion increasingly divides rather than unites us, perhaps there's a case to be made for thinking of our great winter festival, not as specifically a Christian event, but as one of the last great traditions in which we can *all* participate, whatever our beliefs.

---

1 Pascal's wager appears in his *Pensées*, trans. A. J. Krailsheimer (Harmondsworth: Penguin Books, 1966), pp. 149–55.
2 Ludwig Wittgenstein, *Remarks of Frazer's Golden Bough*, ed. Rush Rees, trans. Raymond Hargreaves and Roger White (Oxford: Basil Blackwell, 1975), p. 4.
3 Ibid.
4 Peter Singer, *How Are We to Live?* (Oxford: Oxford University Press, 1996), pp. 118–9.